A Distillation of Hills

The author on Steeple Summit above Ennerdale
August 1989

A Distillation of Hills

David J. Lythgoe

Chapeltown Books

British Library Cataloguing in Publication Data

A Record of this Publication is available from the British Library

ISBN 978-1-910542-92-7

Photography by David J. Lythgoe
Cover design © Alan Prosser

Cover: The hills of Assynt, Canisp, Suilven,
Cul Mor, Cul Beag and Stac Pollaidh from Sidhean Mor

This edition published 2022 by Chapeltown Books
Manchester, England

Alas that the longest hill
Must end in a vale; but still
Who climbs with toil, whereso'er
Shall find wings waiting there.

Henry Charles Beeching 1859-1919

CONTENTS

ILLUSTRATIONS

FOREWORD BY NICK BARRETT

Lessons learned and experiences gained in the outdoors can endure for life. At Outward Bound, during the relatively short time participants are in our care, they develop lifelong skills, such as teamwork and resilience, sound decision making and a healthy relationship with risk and adventure. We are privileged to witness how people absorb their environment and surroundings and create pathways to lifelong connection and passion.

Time spent walking is time well spent. The conservationist and explorer John Muir wrote 'the mountains are calling, and I must go' and it is the unique and rugged terrain of the Lakes that has been calling walkers of all ages and abilities to experience their charms for centuries. The hills provide a place for solitary expedition as well as group experience; a sense of space and belonging, a place to contemplate and enjoy.

In this book, we are invited to experience one man's extensive memories of a lifetime of walking, whilst reflecting on our own. The influences of course U22 at the Outward Bound Mountain School in Ullswater in the autumn of 1957 have clearly created a platform on which this passion is founded, and we are very pleased to have played a small part in this journey.

Nick Barrett, Outward Bound CEO, 2006 –

PREFACE

During the first Covid lockdown, finding that I had an unprecedented amount of spare time, I thought I might select from a lifetime of walking and climbing hills and mountains, those walks and climbs that I thought were my ten most enjoyable. I intended the list to be only for my own pleasure, but when I began to sift through piles of diaries, photographs and loose documents, I began to remember not only events, but also faces and places that I couldn't bring myself to exclude. I needed to record far more than a simple list.

I soon had to revise exactly what I meant by 'most enjoyable'. Some walks were enjoyed because they were shared with friends, others because I walked alone. Some were on days of glorious sunshine while others were spent in uncomfortable, miserable and soul-destroying rain. Some had been planned in advance; others were decided on the spur of the moment. In short, I wanted to record not only a bare account of what I climbed or where I walked, but also my companions and my emotions. I wanted to taste again the clear water of a mountain stream, to see again the glint of sunlight falling on virgin snow, to feel again a biting wind on my face and hear again the haunting call of the curlew, the plaintive cry of the buzzard or the song of a skylark rising to heaven. I wanted to recall the joys, the surprises, the fears, the exhilaration and the suspense of wondering what lay beyond the next hill.

Gradually, I realised that my simple list had developed into a mini-autobiography that I could use at any time to recall, not only the freedom of a fellside uncluttered by the demands of a busy world, but also the satisfaction of achieving a goal despite the aching limbs and the complaining lungs.

But most of all, I knew in the end that I wanted to share my walks and climbs with those millions of walkers and climbers who, like me, don't know why they do it. And they probably never will, because the never ending call of the hills is a mystery that defies explanation.

D.J.L.

INTRODUCTION

One cool, wet day in August 1960 I was alone and hanging by one hand from a hold on the top pitch of Broad Stand on Scafell about thirty feet above a slope of shattered scree. To be in such a situation concentrates the mind wonderfully. If I hadn't observed the cardinal rule of rock climbing, always to have three points of contact with the rock before moving the fourth, I would not be writing this. I was wearing Vibram rubber soled boots and climbing wet rock alone and I should have known better. But hills and mountains have always called me strongly with a mystical power that I can't explain. Of course I've had my dreams of climbing the Matterhorn, Nanga Parbat, Everest or Kanchenjunga, but (with two exceptions recorded in the pages that follow) for various reasons I've never had an opportunity to explore beyond the confines of these islands. Like many children, I found great delight in climbing and I explored the boundaries of my world from an early age. I can only suppose that my parents must have remembered their own childhood desires and allowed me more freedom than I seem to remember was given to my playmates. Or maybe the reason is simply that some of us are born with a wandering gene.

At the start of the second world war, I was two years old and an only child. Not that I was lonely, but my father would disappear from the family home for weeks at a time and it was much later that I learned that he'd enlisted with the Volunteer Defence Force, later to become the Home Guard, and had to travel the length and breadth of the country for training purposes. He would later travel the world as a British soldier and only return home (from Singapore) in 1946.

During the war we shared the Anderson shelter in the back yard of our terraced house with our next-door neighbours, but it was a cold, damp and uninviting refuge and I only remember it being used once, even though air raid warnings would sound occasionally – there was a Royal Ordnance factory a quarter of a mile away, but nothing else locally to attract a German bomb except the main West coast railway line. After my dad left home to join the army, I was raised by mum who had to contend with the privations of wartime rationing and restrictions. Luxuries were few and I only realised much later in life how much my mother had sacrificed on my behalf and how much as a child I took for granted. We were not a rich family in terms of wealth, but we had riches beyond compare in love and understanding from friends, family and neighbours.

Mum and Dad had taught me to read before I started school, so apart from listening to the radio on which the programmes were mostly happy, bright and cheerful, no doubt dictated by the government, I found my escape from the strictures of daily life by reading anything I could lay my hands on – especially adventure stories. Robin Hood was my first undoubted favourite, to be followed by Robinson Crusoe. I soon discovered the writings of H. Rider Haggard and Robert Louis Stevenson, especially *King Solomon's Mines*, *Treasure Island* and *Kidnapped* and I was enchanted by tales of pirates and their exploits. I joined the local library and soon exhausted everything that interested me in the children's section, only to be greatly affronted when the librarian refused me permission to pass through a barrier to get at the adult books.

But by then I had discovered names such as Scott of the Antarctic, Grenfell of Labrador and Captain James Cook, not to mention Mallory and Irvine who both sadly died on Everest. Such were the explorers and pioneers that were the major influences on my young life, and while I could never hope to emulate their adventures, I could at least live them in my dreams. I can't recall how old I was, but I do remember that when I received my first World Atlas, I was disappointed to find that there were apparently no blanks on the maps remaining to be explored. Of course, I was wrong, but my childhood dreams of becoming a famous explorer had been shattered.

So this book is written for readers who have never lost their childhood curiosity and would like to be reminded of how it feels to discover and explore new worlds, either beyond the visible far horizons or the hidden worlds that live as metaphors inside the mind. It is not a book about an intrepid machete toting explorer slashing his way through jungles. It is not about the highest peaks on the seven continents, nor does it describe a solo circumnavigation of the world. It isn't even about a collector of Scottish Munros, although some of those delectable mountains will be encountered within its pages. Rather, it is for everyone who loves hills, mountains and wild places and cannot live without the distant view. If it stimulates the reader to remember their own adventures recalling again the force of the wind, the sting of the rain or the warmth of the sun, then so much the better.

There were few trees amongst the terraced streets where I lived and those in the municipal park were out of bounds for aspiring climbers; the park wardens were too vigilant. One of my junior school classmates lived in a house where the garden included a huge tree located in Sycamore Drive. This was the first tree I remember climbing so it may have been a sycamore of moderate size. It may not have been a great height, but it remains lodged in the memory because I climbed until I feared the swaying of the thin leading branch, responding to my tiny weight, might break. I tore off a scrap of bark as proof of how far I'd climbed and for the first time in my short life I exercised prudence and climbed down. But I had seen far beyond a row of garden fences, experienced the thrill (and fear) of reaching my limits and had learnt, without realising, that somewhere in the future I would travel further and climb higher.

It was not long before I did, for in 1947, following the death of Lord Crawford, his grand house and estate, known locally as the Haigh Plantations, was bought for the town by Wigan Council. My uncle, who was employed by the Council told me that I could now explore this previously forbidden land without fear of being apprehended by a minion of the law. It was within walking distance of my home, so I was soon to be found there exploring alone on Saturday mornings, although I remember distinctly my first tentative passage through the imposing gateway, expecting at any moment to have my collar metaphorically fingered by a policeman. This to me was William Brown country as described by Richmal Crompton, whose books I was devouring as fast as I could get hold of them. On one occasion I found the front entrance to the hall to be open and silently crept inside. There was no one about so I climbed a grand staircase to a gallery where a host of multicoloured keys and trowels was displayed inside a glass cabinet. Somewhere at the far end of the building I could hear whistling, presumably a workman going about his business. I found another door, opened it as quietly as I could and behind it discovered a spiral staircase. For a moment I was "Just William" reborn and climbed the spiral to where it opened on to the roof. That was far enough, for the longer I stayed the greater was the danger of being caught.

With a rapidly thumping heart I manged to escape undetected and made my way through a tangle of overgrown rhododendrons to a wooden tower on the highest point of the estate. I have since supposed that it was used by His Lordship to fly his flag and so advertise to the local populace that he was in residence. Not surprisingly, it was surrounded by a metal fence, but judging by its condition someone had clearly been there before me. I squeezed through and climbed a series of ladders from floor to floor inside until I emerged on to the roof with an extensive view over the forest canopy to Rivington Pike in one direction and the infamous "Three Sisters" conical colliery waste tips beyond Wigan in the other. The tower must have been demolished soon after my visit because I never saw it again. I assume that the authorities must have been considered it to be dangerous, especially to small adventurous children.

I had then no knowledge of hills, not even the hills of Britain, and certainly not mountains but I began to seek out such high points as I could find. Two of these were close to home and on opposite sides of the main North West railway line close to my home in Wigan. For obvious reasons the higher one was known locally as Scout's Hill and the lower as Cub's Hill. Both consisted of waste from what had once been coal pits, but they were then a magnet for every local child and I soon found them. Maybe they were no higher than fifty feet or so above the surrounding fields, but for a small child they were as desirable as the Matterhorn must have been to Edward Whymper. In winter they took on alpine proportions.

Lord Crawford's wooden flagstaff tower
c.1948

From that time, wherever there was something to climb, be it a tree, a lamp post a fence or a wall I would climb it. Few memories remain from those years but I remember distinctly a church visit to the Edgworth National Children's Home (NCH) located in the village of Crowthorne on the very edge of the Pennine moors above

17

Bolton. The nearest height of any significance close to Wigan is Rivington Pike at 1033 ft above sea level but being 10 miles away it was then too far to travel for an impecunious child and it had to wait until I possessed a bicycle. Before the day of the NCH visit I had discovered, on an Ordnance Survey map, a spot height about a mile distant from the Home with the name Bull Hill at 1372 ft above sea level. While the adults were given a conducted tour of the Home, I led two of my young companions on an excursion to find this dot on the map. But it was a day of continuous rain and once we had turned off a reasonable cart track, we were soon squelching miserably through ankle deep peat bogs wearing our everyday school shoes. We never reached the summit (if there was one) and no doubt I was severely reprimanded for such silly behaviour.

Perhaps I have an innate sense of insecurity, for I always seem to need to know two things – my place in time and my place in space. Without this information I often feel that I am both literally and metaphorically lost. I am at a loss to explain this. Most people seem to get by without any such worries. In an unfamiliar location they can always find someone to guide them in the right direction. Maybe there ought to be a phrase or word to describe my condition. Locotemporophobia perhaps. Whatever the case, since my earliest memory, maps have fascinated me. The single adornment to the wall of my childhood bedroom was a simple map showing all the main line railway routes throughout Britain delineated in red. I bought it from a second-hand book stall for a pittance with my meagre pocket money, but it remained my pride and joy for many years until I left the parental home for one of my own. That map was a far better investment than a bar of chocolate.

At school, a magnificent globe of the world was suspended from the ceiling of the geography room. That, together with a Bartholemew's World Atlas and those marvellous creations of the Ordnance Survey Office reinforced in me an interest in maps that has never diminished. Possibly the fanciful depiction of Robert Louis Stevenson's Treasure Island, together with the fact that, from the whole of the British Isles, Mr. Bartholemew had selected my local area to illustrate differences in rainfall, lent an added magic to his atlas. I have never forgotten his colourful maps of the continents, in particular that of South America on which the Amazon basin featured strongly in dark green. He described it as being one of the "lungs of the world". The immensity of that area and the current rate of its on-going destruction convinces me that for the past fifty years or so we have been irresponsible curators of this beautiful planet. Climate changes and global warming are phenomena that can no longer be denied. They must surely, in part, be caused by the destruction of the forests of the Amazon basin.

But enough of politics. For me, at school there was something about the cabalistic symbols of Ordnance Survey maps that appealed more than a second language, although from the viewpoint of an unbeliever, that was exactly what they were, and no doubt still are. Interpreting contour lines allowed me to develop a three-dimensional picture of a landscape that was invisible to the uninitiated. Roads that were usually depicted then as red, brown or yellow lines, would lead me over hills into undiscovered valleys so that in my mind's eye I could visualise every rise and fall and hairpin bend. Railways either ran through cuttings or were raised high on embankments, and shorelines were either sandy or rocky.

When I acquired a Raleigh Sports bicycle and could explore beyond the walking limits of my two short legs, my joy was almost complete. I added a mileometer to the front wheel that clicked annoyingly, but reassuringly, as I covered thousands of miles travelling the length and breadth of South Lancashire – and many miles beyond. Of course. Rivington Pike was soon added to my pathetic little list of summits and although I soon completed a circuit of Pendle Hill, a round trip of about 80 miles, the hill itself would only succumb a few years later.

Such were my formative years when I would enjoy long days cycling to Llangollen and the Horseshoe Pass (125 miles) or the Lake District (145 miles) but with too little time to complete the ascent of a mountain. But, although the big hills continued to beckon, a couple more years would pass before I ascended

Snowdon, the first of many subsequent names that I considered to be real mountains.

Aged fifteen and with my school friend, John Shepherd, I crossed the Pennines to the Yorkshire coast, cycling every day for a week between youth hostels – but no summits were gained on that trip other than that of the road over Blackstone Edge.

I guess it was no accident that having such an affinity with maps, I would eventually (probably too old) take up the pursuit of fell-running. In addition to being able to read a map with the same pleasure that other people read a good book, in middle age, I needed to become fit. "A healthy mind in a healthy body" goes the mantra that persuaded me to begin my (self-imposed) training using local maps on a scale that allowed me to plot a variety of routes, stitching together footpaths that included as much countryside as I could find with the inevitable necessity of running on urban streets.

Finally, maps have always provided me with more than basic information. They provide me now with a delicious nostalgia that warms the heart and soothes the brain. They bring to mind those sweet days of summer when sunshine clothed the mountain tops and the view stretched to infinity. As an ex-fell runner, with the aid of a map, without leaving my chair, I can still trace the course of a mountain stream and recall its every twist and turn – the spot where an adder slept on a sun warmed rock, or the moment when a sudden break in the mist revealed a view that took my breath away. In the cold depths of winter, I can happily turn off the TV and warm myself by merely opening a map. By this simple act I can reflect on the lung bursting pain of a steep ascent or the sensation of sheer joy that I came to know when descending a grassy path as if I had winged feet. Of such is the joy of maps.

A Lancashire Landscape

My home town of Wigan has a long and honourable history, having been granted by Henry III in 1247 a charter to hold a market. The town expanded rapidly during the industrial revolution because of its dependence on the 3 Cs – coal, cotton and canals. It may pre-date the Romans as a settlement because the oldest part of the town stands on raised ground where the foundations of a substantial Roman bath house have been excavated within a loop of the River Douglas (loosely translated as "black water"). During the 19th and early 20th centuries the ubiquity of the coal pits that surrounded the town was enough to sully every building in the town with a thin layer of coal dust. There were many hills of waste left behind when the pits closed and from the front bedroom window of my home I could see three conical mountains in the distance known as the "Three Sisters". They were razed to the ground many years ago and are commemorated today in the name of the Three Sisters Country Park. The following poem describes the town in which I grew up.

Do you know the town where I used to live
where Saturday men raced scrawny dogs.
Where streets would ring to the sound of clogs,
and a thousand chimneys choked me with fogs?

Do you know the grey hill where I used to sit
watching open wagons shunt coal from the pit?
Beyond those sidings, I knew far away
more hills of grey would be growing each day.

Do you know the fields where I used to play
with winding gear that was always near
and the whistle that blew so that everyone knew
it was the end of a shift? Unless it meant fear!

Do you know the street where I used to walk
every day to the shop for a loaf of bread,
where a spectacled man looked kindly down
and ruffled the hair on a small boy's head?

Do you know the park where I used to ride
on a roundabout, scraping my shoes in the mud,
or the path that led me into a wood
where the scream of a partridge froze my blood?

Those hills of my childhood are now all laid low
and it's hard to remember I once used to go
to the hills with a bucket to pick nuggets of coal
when mother was pregnant and dad on the dole.

They have taken and levelled my memories for good
of the miners who dug for the shiny black gold.
No footprints are left where the old pithead stood
and widows in mourning could not be consoled.

All the wagons have left now that kept me from sleep,
though I hear their clanking still loud in my dreams,
and the hollowed out earth has its secrets to keep
in the loveless cold arms of the empty dead seams.

Now immaculate streets will forever deny
those forgotten grey clinkers of cinders and waste,
for the sweat ridden landscapes that once saw men die,
by green fields and woodlands have all been replaced.

JOHN SHEPHERD

John and I were in the same class at Wigan Grammar School. During our second year there, both of us aged twelve, Wigan town council decided to carry out a car parking survey. By chance we were paired together to patrol certain streets and record car registration numbers. From that time, we became close friends, and it was John, possibly sensing that we were kindred spirits, who suggested that we walk one Saturday to Rivington Pike and back, a total distance of about 16 miles. We had previously walked about ten miles to St. Helens where his father was working and we returned by car, but I had worn ordinary shoes and developed painful blisters. This time I would wear my gym shoes and by evening I was thankful that I had.

The day was warm but not hot and it was dark before 9.00 pm when we arrived home so it must have been an early autumn day, probably soon after the start of another school year. We had used the Haigh Plantations as a short cut and the gloom under the trees, which were then much denser than today, made progress rather difficult, especially when, in the darkness, we stumbled over a hedgehog. Haigh Plantations had only become available to the people of Wigan in 1947 and were a favourite playground for me. Because I lived nearer than John, I had already explored the many paths, ponds and recesses of what then had turned into natural wild country, for the wooded estate had been left uncultivated for many years and nature had reclaimed the estate for herself. I was able to introduce John to the many delights of this (almost) private adventure park. Often, and as frequently as time allowed, we struggled or hacked our way through the dense undergrowth of rhododendrons, to find streams, ponds and bogs and an unexpected miniature railway line. We climbed rock walls, discovered waterfalls and followed paths that led us over bridges to a promised land of pure delight.

Unlike many of my schoolmates I had never received a bicycle when I passed the 11+ exam. I'd never had any such expectation,

23

but I received one for my 13th birthday. This was to become my passport to lands far and away beyond my dreams. Rivington Pike and Lord Lever's estate were now within reach of an evening's ride so John and I soon extended our explorations and would ride out there on a summer's evening and try either to climb the ivy on the walls of the Liverpool Castle replica or explore the many paths through a more demanding estate than the one at Haigh. Here on the steep hillside were stone steps and buildings, more waterfalls, bridges and, miraculously and unexpectedly on such a steep slope, we discovered ornamental lakes hiding amongst the trees.

In the year that we both turned fifteen, John had the idea of cycling across England from Wigan to Bridlington on the east coast, the latter because it had a youth hostel. We were both old enough and eligible to join the Youth Hostels Association (YHA). There was also a hostel at York and John had a cousin who lived in Bradford who was willing to let us stay overnight on our outward and return journeys. My mum and dad, although no doubt apprehensive at the thought of their beloved son and his friend embarking on such an adventure at such a tender age, eventually consented with the proviso that I should send a postcard from each overnight stop along the way. For someone whose only holiday had previously been a week at Scarborough, this would be a magical week, even though we encountered severe head winds as we climbed the hills to Blackstone Edge to cross the Pennines, were reprimanded by a policeman in Halifax for jumping a red light (he relented when we explained our mission and asked him for directions) and rode the wrong way along a one way street in York, (fortunately unobserved by the keepers of the law).

This was the first time that I had travelled anywhere significant without being overseen by my loving parents and it gave me a taste for travel that, sub-consciously I think I already knew I had. My Raleigh Lenton Sports cycle with its drop handlebars was more than merely a means of transport. It was my passport to a greater world than I had ever known. I devoured books on travel with an insatiable hunger and read everything I could lay my hands on from the local library.

Youth Hostel Association Handbook, 1952

When I was once asked by a school mate why I was reading about Snowdon, having never been there, I replied that when the time came to ascend that mountain, I would have no need of a map because I had already ascended it many times in my imagination – and by several diverse paths.

I was destined soon to do exactly that. When Everest was climbed in 1953, John and I went to the Ritz cinema in Wigan one Saturday afternoon where the film of the expedition was showing. We sat and watched *The Conquest of Everest* twice, if not three times because, once seated, we could stay all day to watch the same film again and again. Whether or not such behaviour was strictly legal I have no idea, but we were never ejected.

The last memory that I have of sharing an adventure with John is during the last summer holidays that we spent together. John's family was catholic and, having been with his parents to Lourdes, he returned, seemingly having grown by about six inches. Although surprised, I accepted this as a fact, as well as the pen-knife that he gave me as a present from his foreign travels – something that I could not reciprocate. We were paired, at that time to continue a system that had been set up to record, on a daily basis, the weather at the school, even during the school holidays. John and I were allocated our specific week (or it may have been weeks) and we duly attended the supposedly closed school as expected.

This was, for me, and I expect also for John, a chance to go where we had never been and having unrestricted and legitimate access, we ascended to the roof of the school clock tower. In retrospect, anyone might have done as we did, but would not subsequently crawl along the cat-walk above the school assembly hall and poke a hole through the ceiling with a recently acquired pen knife. This was a gross abuse of our privilege. Viewed from the floor of the hall, the resulting scar resembled nothing more than a black fly, but the sin has haunted me from that day to this and will no doubt continue to do so.

After completing A-levels in maths, physics and chemistry I left school and went straight into industry as a trainee chemist in the laboratory of Wigan's Westwood Power station. The interview for the post was held on my last day at school so I missed the poignant last assembly and the chance to say goodbye to all my teachers and friends. I only saw John once after that and although much later I called at his old address to renew our acquaintance, it was only to learn that the family had moved away and nobody could tell me to where. So it was with much regret that much later, when returning from a foreign holiday, I read his obituary in the Wigan Observer, a local paper for which he had been chief editor.

For John

One Saturday morning,
'Let's walk to Rivington Pike,' he said.
A distant nipple breasting the Pennine
fringe ten miles away. School plimsolls,
sandwiches and fairy cakes.
Welfare orange juice.
A torch.
Unseen pheasants brayed. Afraid.
'This land is private. Turn back
and find another way.'
We arrived forgetting blistered feet. Found
a widespread waste of fire blighted moor.
Dead heather clutching the peat.

Shadows stretched their limbs
across our homeward path. Pink
underskirts of clouds above. Birds closing
eyes on rafters of trees. In the dark
we stumbled on a ball of spikes.
At last John's torch had proved its worth.

FIRST MOUNTAIN

Between leaving school and starting work, there was time enough for me to be included in a family holiday to spend a week in a caravan at Towyn in North Wales. For me, the big attraction was that sometime during the week I might have a chance to climb Snowdon. During the same week, my cousin John was with his family in a neighbouring caravan. Being related, both families were close and tended to spend much time together, so when they suggested a joint trip to Caernarfon Castle, I casually mentioned the idea that John and I might do a traverse of Snowdon. Although the adults might have thought this to be a spontaneous thought, I had been reading Ward Lock's Guide to North Wales and had studied the appropriate half inch Bartholemew map. On a good day I knew with the arrogance of youth that there should be no difficulty following the Snowdon Ranger path that starts from the youth hostel of that name near Llyn Cwellyn and ascends easily to the summit. We would then descend using the Pyg track to the hostelry of Pen-y-Pass at the top of the Llanberis valley.

Maybe John and I were fortunate to have parents who understood the desire of their children to explore a world about which they themselves knew nothing, but such a golden opportunity had never before come my way. I was very persuasive as I explained the care that we would take with regard to safety, and I don't recollect there being much opposition to my proposals. At about 2.00 pm John and I were dropped off at Snowdon Ranger youth hostel. Because there was only one map, I thought it best to leave it with the adults and for their benefit even marked the reunion point with a large X. How arrogant and condescending was that! There had been near continuous rain all that week, but this day had dawned with clear skies and would remain so. I had estimated the crossing would take us under four hours but told the adults to allow an extra thirty minutes before they contacted the mountain rescue services if we failed to turn up at 6.00 pm.

No doubt we had placed ourselves at the mercy of Providence.

Not for the first time a casual observer might have thought that we were ill equipped for such a venture. We were both wearing plimsolls, shorts and shirts, although each of us carried a pullover, camera and food (in case of emergency!). We had no compass, no boots, no anoraks, no whistle and neither of us had previously been higher than the top of Blackpool Tower. Nor had we ever been near a real mountain in our lives and had still not seen the summit of Snowdon (a ridge hides it from the roadside), and yet I didn't believe we were foolhardy for, as I had boasted earlier that year when challenged at school about my reading, I had the map in my head and the weather was set fair; we were travelling light and were both very fit – we would make good time. Our two families had the only map and would need it to find the proposed rendezvous at Pen-y-Pass. They watched as we climbed the zig-zags on the spur of Foel Goch until we were about to disappear from their view. As we turned a corner, we gave them a last wave. Moments later we saw before us a vast plateau dotted with sheep and our first never to be forgotten view of the tremendous western flank of the mountain.

To one who had never seen such majesty, the view was awe inspiring in its immensity; even the summit café was not recognised for what it is. 'How long to the summit?' asked John. 'About an hour,' I replied casually, but really without any idea at all. The track became indistinct in places but was easy enough to follow as far as the steep ground that lies above and to the right of the Clogwyn D'ur Arddu crags where only rock climbers dare to go. Those slopes were an obvious target.

We kept to the drier ground wherever possible but at one point stopped at a stream and for the first of many such occasions emulated the selected men of Gideon's army by raising our cupped hands to our lips to drink rather than stoop down and bend our heads, so influential had been this story a part of our biblical education. At one point the track appeared to make a peculiar change of direction but I carried straight on, only to realise that doing so led us straight into a bog. That was my first lesson in practical mountain craft: The apparently direct route on a mountain is not necessarily the easiest or the quickest. Gradually, the path steepened and it seemed that in no time at all we had reached the mountain railway track between Llanberis and the summit.

The view from the summit was all that I had hoped for, and maybe even more so, the ridge on one side leading to Lliwedd and on the other to Crib Goch. The huge bulk of Mynydd Mawr reared up from the far shore of Llyn Cwellyn to the west and in the east, Moel Siabod shimmered in the heat of the late afternoon. We sat a little way below the summit cairn marvelling at the ridge and pinnacles of Crib Goch and the near vertical crags of Lliwedd. We ate our sandwiches and chocolate and threw crumbs to the seagulls circling below our feet. At 4.45 pm I reckoned it was time to be off, for we had the Pyg track and its infamous zig-zags to descend.

Lliwedd from Snowdon summit
July 1954.

By then we were fully attuned to the scale of the mountain architecture which had hit us like a thunderbolt on our first sight of Snowdon a mere two hours earlier. In a state of mild euphoria we thought little of the dangers as we ran down the zig-zags and I totally forgot my promise to take care until John slipped on a wet rock. Fortunately, no damage was done, but it was a salutary lesson and we pressed on more slowly, stopping occasionally to marvel at the mighty cliffs of Lliwedd now closer and towering above us.

So far, we had kept to the correct path but where it seemed to go through a narrow pass in the lower part of what I guess was Crib Goch, we went astray and found ourselves in a wilderness of broken rock and bog. As I went over the ankles in soft mud, Pen-y-Pass came into sight a mere half mile away. We made for the road about 200 yards down on the Llanberis side and reached the car park to find anxious parents scouting for us up the Miners Track. The time was 6.05 pm and I knew then that it would not be long before I returned to climb Snowdon again. Two years later John and I would spend two weeks in the area, including an ascent of Snowdon from Beddgelert by way of Yr Aran as part of a Snowdonia tour.

CONISTON OLD MAN

In the same year that John and I climbed Snowdon, I left school to enter the adult world of work on the 16th of August at Westwood Power Station in Wigan. This was two weeks earlier than the rest of the annual apprentice intake because I was recruited as a trainee industrial chemist. If I hadn't done so, for those two weeks the chief chemist would have been running the laboratory alone. One of his two chemists in training was taking a long-awaited holiday and I was there to replace the other who had taken up a lucrative appointment managing the fresh water supply for the incredibly wealthy ruler of Kuwait on the Persian Gulf. Furthermore, the post of senior assistant chemist was also vacant.

Every year, the British Electricity Authority (BEA), as it was then known, ran an induction course for its new employees at the YMCA centre at Lakeside on Windermere. This was an unexpected bonus for one who was already in love with the area, despite having had only a day visit to the Lake District in the family car to Newby Bridge at the southern end of Windermere. The BEA course consisted mostly of a series of lectures to introduce its new employees to the various aspects of power generation and the complexities of distributing electricity to remote parts of the country. Other lectures were clearly designed to develop self-awareness and social conscience. But the one event that made the week worthwhile for me was a trip by coach to Coniston to ascend Coniston Old Man.

One aspect of the ascent, however, I now believe had not been adequately researched. I don't recall if we were given any instructions about safety on mountains, or even what to do in the event of an accident or emergency. But it's quite possible that in my excitement I wasn't listening. I've since supposed that we were expected to stay together as one long crocodile, all walking at the same pace and always in sight of our leaders. But of course, we youngsters came from a variety of backgrounds. Some would be fearful of the challenge ahead of them; some would do whatever they were told, while others, like myself, would relish the experience.

It was a day of louring clouds, intermittent rain, swollen streams and mist that swirled unpredictably around us. I don't know how many adults were in charge of those ninety or so teenagers, but I recall that I was soon out of touch with most of those ahead of me, as well as those behind. The cloud base was barely above the level of Coppermines Valley, from which point I climbed most of the way alone thinking that if I kept going upwards, then I must eventually reach the summit – which of course I did.

It never struck me at the time that I might end up on the wrong mountain. But there was a clear enough path all the way which I have since seen deteriorate disastrously in its upper reaches. On the way, I encountered for the first time, and most unexpectedly, a body of water which I wasn't expecting at such a height. I didn't know then that it was the mountain tarn that goes by the oxymoronic name of Low Water, although I admit that it lies a few hundred feet lower than the summit of the Old Man at an altitude of about 1900 ft. When I reached the summit, I found only a lone stranger huddled behind the summit cairn, sheltering from driving rain that was actually being blown up hill. Until then I'd been accustomed to rain falling from above so that was another new experience for me. I didn't recognise the refugee from the rain so he may or may not have been one of our leaders but he assured me that even in the mist, if I set off on the correct line, the descent would be no problem (not that I was worried anyway) – I have always had an overweening, though sometimes misplaced, confidence in my ability to survive and find my way home.

Because I had no clothing other than my school gabardine mackintosh and was wearing ordinary everyday shoes (and probably my grammar school cap), by the time I returned to the coach, along with the others, I was soaked to the skin, and along with many of them, I shivered uncontrollably as the coach windows steamed up with condensation all the way back to the YMCA centre where the blessed relief of a hot shower awaited.

That was not the best conceived part of my introduction to the BEA but it was an affirmation of all that I had hoped for. I had enjoyed every minute of the climb – unlike some who swore they would never again set foot on a mountain. Coniston Old Man was my second mountain, but the weather was almost as far removed from that during my ascent of Snowdon as it was possible to be. Consequently. I learned more about mountain weather that day than any amount of book reading would have taught me. Perhaps it was simply good luck that there were no accidents or emergencies because everyone returned safely.

First Times

At seventeen, I faced the world head down
ignoring contour lines. I pedalled hard.
It seemed I never moved as wave
on wave of hills flowed swiftly by
beneath my clicking wheels. They
stretched into a paper plain,
unseen somewhere behind
my carefree piston driven heels
until I stopped to rest in Langdale, where
a man too old for hurry talked of hills
which I had only known by name.
How much I wish today I could recall those
first times when, for me, on foot, the earth
stood still in Wasdale, Eskdale, Borrowdale.

Today, I envy those who've yet to rest by
Loughrigg Tarn or climb Jack's Rake. Whose
futures lie in clouded skies and rain soaked
reddened cheeks. How much I envy
those I'll tell one day about the glorious Jaws
of Borrowdale, and how I shared with
rainbow trout one summer afternoon,
the pools beneath the double bridge
at Grange, one first delicious time.

34

A LAKE DISTRICT CIRCUIT (1)

When I started work, holidays were taken in arrears of days worked, so I had to wait until the following year before I could take a week off. I was still reading everything I could find about climbing and mountaineering. For sentimental reasons I still possess the first book that I bought, funded by my first pay packet which I dutifully handed to Mum and Dad, (I was earning £2 -9s - 9d per week). The title, not surprisingly, is *Chambers Illustrated Guide and Souvenir to the Lake District*. I was also using the local library and discovered works by the blessed W. A. Poucher from which I learnt much about equipment. I quote his advice *"Anyone who ventures on the hills without proper equipment is asking for trouble and since the weather is one of our greatest hazards it is wise to be prepared... by wearing proper boots and clothing..."* He goes on at length and mentions vibram soles and the need to take the utmost care to avoid a slip. I absorbed everything without question and, having arranged to take my cousin John for a week youth hostelling round the Lake District, I ensured that we would wear strong boots (that we nailed ourselves) and carry spare food (emergency rations), plenty to drink, extra clothing against inclement weather, a change of stockings, a change of shoes, a suitable map, a compass, a sheet sleeping bag (a requirement of the YHA), and a simple first aid kit. For a week in England in July, I thought that we wouldn't need an aneroid barometer or an ice-axe, but I did take a camera.

In the summer of 1955, my dad drove us to Windermere (the town, not the lake) and with bulging rucksacks we set off to climb Orrest Head using the map in Ward Lock's *Guide to the Lakes*. It was a hot day and every day that week would be the same. We soon cursed the extra food and clothing that were never needed on the subsequent long dry climbs when the burning sun beat mercilessly down, but that first day was a short one and no more than a gentle stroll, although I had a moment of panic (being the leader) when we dropped down to a road to see the hostel nestling amongst trees on the far side of a deep valley that contained a substantial river. Luckily, after consulting the map, we found a foot bridge and were soon at the hostel. The next day, my diary records that we effectively walked across the Sahara desert. Expecting the day to be hot, we completed our chores (a requirement of the YHA in those days) early, and set off up the Garburn Pass, a gentle, tree-shaded slope that in its lower reaches was pleasant underfoot. But the higher we climbed the more the trees thinned out and when we turned off the track to Kentmere to make for the summit of Yoke, there was no shade at all and we paid dearly in toil and sweat. We had a short rest on top of Yoke and stopped again on Ill Bell where we dined on youth hostel sandwiches. We each had a bottle of cream soda but no bottle opener. Bad mistake!

We were now making for Patterdale with nothing to drink. In my inexperience I had supposed that there would be streams of life-giving water along the ridge over Ill Bell and Froswick to Thornthwaite Crag and High Street. There were not. If there had been one single pool of fetid water we would have sucked it dry. But from The Knott, we spied Hayes Water and with not a moment lost we sped like mountain goats, hurtling down the steep slopes with never a care for life or limb and we drank until we were fit to burst.

Now there is a method of opening a metal capped bottle if no opener is to hand. One firmly holds the bottle top against a solid surface such as a table edge and with the other hand one gives the wrist a sharp blow. This may work under ideal conditions but not when the only hard edge belongs to a semi-stable, badly angled rock. When I tried this technique, hoping for a taste of my cream soda, the neck of the bottle fractured so that I managed to slash my left hand allowing so much blood to run that any passing stranger (there were none of course) would have been horrified at my appearance as blood congealed from hand to elbow in the afternoon heat. We made a hurried decent to Patterdale and found a doctor in Glenridding. The injury to the soft fleshy part of my hand was more inconvenient than painful because from thereon it interfered with my usual method of clutching the straps of my rucksack, especially when toiling up a steep slope.

The weather the next day was identical to the previous one as a burning sun beat down all day from a cloudless sky. This was not the sort of day I would have chosen to hump a heavy rucksack over a 3,000 ft mountain to Keswick. It was a day for lazing among sand hills listening to gentle breakers lapping on a sandy shore. However, as pilgrims will, we went forth to conquer the mighty Helvellyn, a mountain famous for the hazardous ridge of Striding Edge. We took the ascent to the start of the ridge slowly with many stops to re-tie boot laces or admire the view (or so we pretended). The ridge itself presented no problems until we reached the point where it abuts against the great mass of the mountain where a more than usually difficult series of steps forced us off balance due to the weight of our packs.

I had intended to travel North over the Dodds but on reaching Fisherplace Gill, decided it would be better on such a day to descend to the road and endure the fumes of cars and lorries on the road to Keswick rather than the fresh breeze blowing on the tops. At least there would be drinkable water from the stream as far as the road. That fact alone bears testimony to the heat of the day. A road walk is no way to end a climb and Helvellyn remained in my mind for many years as a dry and dusty mountain with no redeeming features. Not even the delightful exposure of Striding Edge could save it on that day.

I had planned the walk from Keswick to the hostel at Black Sail to be an easy day after the rigours of Helvellyn. There were no summits to walk over, the only climb of any note being that to the drum house above Honister Pass. But as we walked the length of Borrowdale we again needed to seek out the shade of every single tree along the road, even at times crossing from one side of the road to the other. My wounded hand was beginning to heal and was less painful, but the climb to the drum house with no shade at all was hard going. But then the wandering track across the slopes of Fleetwith Pike and Haystacks was a delight with its many twists and turns that kept on giving us unexpected views of Buttermere, while never knowing which of the many depressions ahead would reveal the hostel below us in splendid isolation at the head of

Ennerdale. After our evening meal, the air outside was so calm and still that we sat for a long time watching the sun go down in a blaze of glory as shadows lengthened across the length of Ennerdale.

That night was so hot that we slept with the bedroom door open to the fellside. We woke to a flood of more sunshine and a musty smell in the nostrils suggesting that all was not well. The source of the smell was discovered immediately I opened my eyes, for a wandering Herdwick had chosen to join us at some point during the night and was fast asleep in the middle of the bedroom floor. With such a laughable start to the day I knew we were in for the best day of the week.

Again we were away early and though there was no marked path on the map, the view of Great Gable from the hut had allowed me the night before to plan a direct route up a grassy tongue below the northern crags. So entranced was I by the magnificence of the scenery that we seemed to float upwards without effort until we reached the foot of the crags and were forced to turn right towards what I learned later is Beckhead. We were on the deserted summit by 11.00 am and had seen nobody. But we had far to go and could not delay so after I celebrated by lighting a cigarette,(oh dear) we sped down the screes half running, half walking and fifteen minutes later were at Styhead. There we made our first contact of the day with humanity and the spell of solitude was broken.

Our winged feet now gave way to slow plodding along the Guides (now known as the Corridor) route to Scafell Pike. We ate lunch in the most pleasant place we could find with at least a little shade beneath a skeletal rowan tree growing from the side of Greta Gill. We gazed out at Great Gable trying, but failing, to pick out Napes Needle amongst the crags. Resuming our walk, it seemed that Scafell Pike didn't fit with its position on the map until I realised I was looking at Lingmell. I was disappointed to find that the summit of the Pike was crowded. There may have been ten or a dozen people there, which is nothing really compared to the numbers to be found there on such a day nearly 70 years later, so we didn't linger. I remember looking at the stony path over Broad Crag and thinking what a cruel and demanding approach to the Pike it must be.

My cousin John on the Scafell Pike cairn
1955

We descended by Mickledore and Cam Spout easily into upper Eskdale but then began the most gruelling part of the day. We drank deeply from the stream at the foot of Cam Spout but were very soon thirsty again and although the ground was boggy, for the second time that week, we could find no drinkable water as we made innumerable winding and twisting detours across a seemingly endless plateau. We topped a rise only to see another; we turned a corner only to find ourselves confronted by another; the slopes of Slight Side refused to fall behind us and we seemed destined to trudge that burning desert land for evermore. I know now that we were clearly far more dehydrated than we had supposed and another lesson had been learned.

Eventually, we came across a trickle of water which I guess now was a branch of Cowcove Beck, but it so revived our flagging spirits that in no time at all we were on the threshold of Eskdale and were soon in the hostel. Nothing was ever more enjoyable than the cold shower that preceded our dinner. So ended the finest walk of the week and with it a love of the Eskdale valley and the softness of its summer evening light that will stay with me as long as I live.

The heatwave continued the next day as we walked by road, wearing plimsolls rather than boots, over Hardknott and Wrynose passes to the hostel at Elterwater. We had lunch at the Three Shire Stone where the proximity of Pike o' Blisco was enough to tempt me to take John to scamper up to one more summit without having to carry those damned rucksacks. Our last day of a mere five miles was by road to Coniston with plenty of shade, for which we were duly thankful. Again it was so hot that I didn't even have the will to climb the Old Man for a second time, preferring instead to linger all afternoon on the shores of Coniston Water. Indeed we were both exhausted from a week of carrying our loads over some of the highest summits of England, not to mention several other worthy summits as well. But finally, we were beaten by a week of heat from the unrelenting sun. We caught the train home from Coniston the next day discussing plans for the year to come that would turn out to be a two week circuit of Snowdonia.

A SNOWDONIA CIRCUIT

By July 1956, I had been working long enough to be allowed a fortnight's holiday. Again this would be youth hostelling with John but I wanted to cover new ground and so devised a route for a walk in Snowdonia that would last for the whole fortnight. The route was determined firstly by the locations of the youth hostels so I had to plan it as carefully as I had the Lake District circuit the year before. But this time my plan would be to travel round the area clockwise starting from Llanrwst staying for one, two or three nights at each hostel depending on whatever mountains we (that is I) wanted to climb. An additional consideration was that on one day John would rendezvous with his family who would be on holiday at Criccieth. My itinerary for the walk was soon established and would remain unchanged except that at Christmas 1955, I'd met a young girl and hoped that she would be able to join us. Brenda was a nurse in training at the Wigan Royal Albert Infirmary and subject to limited holidays. John had no objection, but Brenda could only join us for the second week when my helpful father would drive her to Llanberis where I had booked three nights for three people.

John and I took the train from Wigan to Llandudno Junction from where we boarded a bus to Llanrwst for our first night. Being in Wales, I suppose I shouldn't have been surprised that the bus conductor serenaded us with a variety of Welsh songs, gave us a running commentary on the customs, vagaries and predilections of the local population and delivered some parcels *en route*. We arrived in Llanrwst with time to visit the church and admire the splendid bridge over the River Conwy attributed to the famous architect, Inigo Jones.

On our first day we walked to Capel Curig by first crossing the river Conwy using the railway bridge (possibly illegally) to a minor road on the far side of the valley where we hoped to find a way through the massed conifers of Gwydir forest. Peacocks were displaying their finery at Gwydir Castle as we searched for the start of the forest path. Eventually, we came across a barrier that was obviously intended to prevent vehicular access, but the track beyond seemed to lead in the right direction so we took it and were almost immediately cocooned in the silence of the forest. All was well with the world until we emerged from the far side of the forest to find a wasteland of peat hags, rocky outcrops and immature plantings. My diary records that *"...we soon lost the abominable path amidst a wilderness of bogs aflame with flies..."* that plagued us continuously. I don't remember there being any semblance of a path for several miles, so I probably set a compass course and hoped for the best as we used whatever spare material we had to cover every square inch of exposed flesh against the invading insects. The weather had changed by then to a day of intermittent drizzle that obscured all the delectable mountains of my desire and was not an auspicious start to the journey.

However, I had read *I Bought a Mountain* by Thomas Firbank who, aged 21, bought the farm of Dyffryn Mymbyr that stands austerely above the road from Capel Curig to Llanberis. From that point on the road a path heads toward the summit of Glyder Fach which was to be our mountain the next day. Sadly, it rained again all that day but we set off in thick mist with high hopes but poor visibility and we did in fact reach our objective, although I wasn't sure at the time, and it wasn't without some poor navigation by me. I learned much that day about keeping my compass always to hand because having climbed to some level ground, we walked steadily across a plateau and passed a small tarn until we reached a point where the ground fell steeply away. We had obviously walked across a broad ridge to its far side, but when the swirling mist cleared for a moment, I saw only a huge valley where I expected Tryfan, a 3,000 ft mountain, to be.

Something was seriously wrong so I got out the compass and could hardly believe it. We were walking 180° contrary to the direction from which we had started and were now looking down at the mountainside that we had climbed earlier that morning. I kept the compass in my hand after that, noting that we passed the tarn again on our other side. A salutary lesson had been learnt and we reached the summit without further trouble but had no distant view through the all-enveloping cloud. Rather than return by the same route we descended, using the compass of course, to the Ogwen road by way of the spur of Gallt Yr Ogof.

The next day I'd hoped that we would climb Moel Siabod but the weather was equally bad so we had a leisurely road walk of five miles to my next planned hostel in the Lledr Valley. Understandably we reached the seemingly haunted looking and apparently deserted but pleasant hostel with time to spare. Three girls who turned up much later were the only other hostellers to stay that night. There was no electricity so we all went to bed by oil lamp.

Apart from the weather, my plans were working well and the next morning we caught the local bus to Blaenau Ffestiniog, leaving it at Tal-y-waeneth to climb two more mountains, Moelwyn Mawr and Cnicht. We were heading to the hostel at Cae Dafydd, not far from Pont Aberglaslyn. The name translates into English as "David's field" which I thought was nicely appropriate for me. The ascent of Moelwyn began through a mountainside of slate debris that we often sent skittering and clattering on its noisy way to the bottom. But the quarries were soon left behind as we found ourselves being drenched by heavy rain (would it never end?) on the bare mountain. The way was pathless but a tremendous ridge curved round to the highest point in sight that I thought would be the summit. It looked as if it would take us an hour to get there but 15 minutes later we were eating our lunch by the cairn with the clouds lifting and the sun breaking through. Hallelujah!

Two ways were now open to us to reach Cnicht – either we dropped 1500 ft to the valley bottom or we contoured some two miles or thereabouts round the head of Cwm Croesor. Our decision was made for us when we came across a line of sleepers from a disused tramway that plunged straight down to the valley floor while the contoured route looked difficult and trackless, even though by using it, we wouldn't lose our hard won height.

By the time we reached the summit of Cnicht, we had dried out and needed a rest. There was a glorious view of the River Glaslyn estuary in the distance and of the tiny village of Croesor, almost immediately below us. Further to the South-west where I'd expected to see the youth hostel there was no sign of any habitation whatsoever, not even a road. As we rested, John asked me, 'Where's the hostel then?'

'I've no idea, but it's somewhere down there amongst those rocky outcrops, ridges and hidden valleys,' I answered.

Cae Dafydd, now a private house but a youth hostel in 1956
Photo by permission May 2021

Cnicht has the soubriquet "The Welsh Matterhorn", more because of its appearance than its difficulties although there are some challenging rocky steps. How we managed to descend the steep ridge while carrying our substantial rucksacks, I've no idea. It was difficult enough when I returned in 2021 (65 years later) to climb it with my daughter, Rosalind, although I then had to take extra care owing to my age, my poor balance and my left femur infirmity (of which more later). I guess John and I would have followed the end of the ridge facing into the rock, so descended the hardest parts with our backs to the estuary until eventually we hit the Welsh "Slate Trail". There we would have turned right towards the scattered village of Nantmor and the youth hostel.

It was while descending from Cnicht, that John and I encountered the only people on the hills we had seen in four days. The evidence of industry amongst those hills is even more pronounced in that corner of Wales than anything in the Lake District and, away from habitation, the country is even wilder. When the summit of Snowdon is awash with tourists who've arrived by mountain railway, these southern hills of Snowdonia present the climber with equally challenging walks and a chance to discover unexpected beauty, even amongst the industrial relics of the past.

But Snowdon was waiting so we made another early start. I was soon to be amazed by the beauty of the view at Pont Aberglaslyn and the charming sound of children's voices singing at Nantmor school as we walked past. With no idea where the Snowdon path started in Beddgelert, we set off somewhere along the Caernarfon road beyond the Saracen's Head hotel passing through what seemed like an interminable succession of allotments and chicken runs until we reached open ground. Once we had left domestication behind, the view began to open up to West and South with Yr Aran looming above us to the East like a miniature Matterhorn.

By then the heat of the day was becoming too much so I abandoned my plans to include Yr Aran and set a direct course for Snowdon itself. By doing so, I had again placed pathless country before us so that we had to endure a dull monotonous slog up an unremitting grassy slope until we came suddenly on the final, more exciting, ridge to the summit. The view when we arrived was through the whole 360° but disappeared almost immediately as a thick and clammy mist descended to envelope us. We tarried but little then and were soon back in sunshine as we descended by the track that we'd climbed two years before from the Snowdon Ranger hostel. After a good night's sleep, the next day we enjoyed an easy walk to Llanberis to meet up with Brenda who, as promised, had been dropped off by my dad.

For our first excursion with Brenda, despite an overcast sky, we took the bus to Pen-y-Pass with the intention of ascending Snowdon by way of Crib Goch. Unfortunately, by the time we'd climbed to the ridge, where we ate our lunch, meanwhile feeding a flock of hungry gulls, the weather had deteriorated so much that I deemed it wise to drop off the ridge to the Miners' Track at the first suitable point. I can't recall how far along the ridge we went, but I guess it would be before the pinnacles, but we were very soon down and walked all the way back along the road to Llanberis, thankful for the relative calm and peace of the valley bottom. The next day was hardly any better. This time we hoped to reach the Idwal Cottage hostel at Llyn Ogwen using the track that by-passes Twll Du (The Devil's Kitchen). We walked along the road again as far as a farm at Beudy Mawr where I expected the hill path to start but a sign "PRIVATE" barred our way.

As we searched up and down the road a gentleman approached us. He was obviously a parson and asked us what we were doing. When I explained that we wished to walk over the ridge by way of the Devil's Kitchen to Idwal Cottage, he was most insistent that we shouldn't do it and told us in a strong Welsh accent that 'There's danger in those hills above.' As if I didn't know! But the weather was steadily deteriorating, mist was down to the valley bottom and it began to rain. I thought back to how I'd led John astray the previous week trying to find Glyder Fach, and in addition, Brenda wasn't looking too happy. Under the circumstances and after some serious thinking I decided I should change my plans. We walked back to Llanberis, bought a loaf and butter, ate lunch, caught the 12.47 bus to Capel Curig and walked the 5 miles by road from there to the top of the Nant Ffrancon pass and the hostel by Llyn Ogwen.

Surely, we thought, by now we must be due for some better weather but the portents were not good. During the night, lightning flashed though the dormitory, thunderbolts echoed from cliff to cliff and rain and hail spattered against the windows. It seemed as if my plans for the Glyders, and possibly Tryfan (added if time allowed), could not go ahead. But by morning the wind had eased and the rain had stopped, although the tops were all in cloud. After

46

a good breakfast we set off along the shore of Llyn Idwal and lingered for a while at the slabs that are a good place for budding rock climbers to learn their trade. I climbed a little way myself and thought them too easy – such arrogance!

Again, we were soon climbing into cloud and ate lunch above the Devils Kitchen on the upper slopes of Glyder Fawr, gradually feeling the cold penetrating such warm clothing as we had on. The further we climbed the colder we became. Peculiarly shaped rocks began to loom up, seemingly a hundred yards away, but within a dozen paces we could touch them. Eventually, and because there seemed to be nowhere higher to climb, we assumed we had reached the summit and so we rested behind a rock out of the wind, watching other rocks appear and disappear through the mysterious shifting mist.

When we had seen enough, we set off for Glyder Fach but suddenly, in the twinkling of an eye the scene changed from a mosaic of black, white and shades of grey into a technicolour world of green grass and blue sky while a brilliant sun warmed us and beat down upon the mile long corridor that had opened up as banks of cloud rolled away on either side of the ridge. Just as suddenly, the mist returned as if unwilling to be defeated and we continued to pursue our solitary way – three travellers lost amongst the ghostly mountains of the moon. Then another gap opened in the curtain of mist to reveal a view down the length of the Nant Ffrancon to Bangor, Anglesey and the Menai with its waters glistening in the sunlight. Then silence and solitude again followed by a further glimpse of beauty, only to have it cut off abruptly as the teasing mist returned. Then another, and another, faster and faster until, as if with a shout of joy, the sun prevailed.

We had thought we were alone but now we saw a multitude of brilliant reds, greens, blues and yellows as people thronged the broad ridge where the cluster of upstanding rocks known as The Castle of the Winds had lost its hiding place. John and I were able to confirm that a week earlier we had indeed reached the summit of Glyder Fach. We then set off for Cwm Tryfan to leave Brenda at the foot of Bristly Ridge while John and I raced up and down

Tryfan taking a mere 30 minutes. There are two huge natural flat-topped monoliths on the summit known to all climbers as Adam and Eve so, still pushing the limits of danger as many have done before, I just had to jump from Adam to Eve (or was it the other way?). I was wearing the boots that I'd nailed myself the previous year and there is a sheer drop waiting for anyone who slips (or skids)! From the A5 road that touches the base of the mountain, motorists often suppose those monoliths to be two people.

We climbed no more hills that week although the weather steadily improved. We had an easy day walking down to Capel Curig on a fine but hazy day to spend our last night of the holiday there. On our final day we walked by forest paths blanketed in pine needles to admire the Swallow Falls from the true left bank of the river and were picked up by dad at Betws-y-Coed that afternoon.

From Pont Aberglaslyn
May 16th 2021

PENDLE HILL FIRST ASCENT

Pendle Hill, from here on referred to simply as "Pendle", is the nearest hill to Wigan of any reasonable height. But being a good thirty miles or so away it remained a target for many years, although I cycled about 80 miles round it soon after my trip with John Shepherd to Bridlington related above. I had met Brenda, my wife to be in 1955 and she had enjoyed walking with my cousin, John, and me on our Snowdonia tour, so in November 1956, when her off-duty was convenient I asked her if she'd like to go with me for my first ascent of Pendle. Doesn't "first ascent" sound grand? But I have always looked upon the first experience of anything in whatever field as either an adventure or a challenge and in some cases as both.

We were both members of the YHA and there was then a youth hostel at Barley, a village at the foot of the hill dominated by its eastern slopes. There was then no bus service to Barley so, having no private means of transport we had to use public bus services from Wigan to Chorley, Chorley to Blackburn and Blackburn to Chatburn. Unfortunately, Chatburn is on the side of Pendle furthest from Barley so we still had a long walk before us and night was closing in before we reached the hostel. Since then, I have often wondered why we didn't use the bus service from Blackburn to Nelson. The walk from there to Barley would have been much shorter. I can only suppose that I was too interested in walking through the pretty village of Downham rather than the terraced streets of an urban town. After dinner that first night, no other hostellers had turned up, so we spent the evening on the common room sofa toasting ourselves before a roaring fire. It was the coldest November weekend for many years and the days, although brilliantly clear, were bitterly cold.

The next day was Remembrance Sunday so we dutifully went to church, as we would have done at home, before we started our climb. The early morning frost, which had been cold and dead in the gloom of the dawn fairly glistened with life and vitality once the sun had risen. We set off by walking past the reservoirs of Ogden Clough. I'd never before been anywhere on the hill except for a hasty up and down walk (and then not to the very top) lasting a half hour during a family outing by car so the whole area was new to me. But I was familiar with the topography from 1. Harrison Ainsworth's *Lancashire Witches.* and 2. *Walks and Talks With Fellman* by E. Williams, a book that I'd bought with my first earnings. I later realised that Mr Williams had lived at what transpired to be the hostel in which we were staying for those two nights in Barley. Whether or not he had been the hostel warden when he wrote his book I've no idea, but a photograph that he included in the book showing him in front of the hostel left me in no doubt that he had once lived there.

It was a bitterly cold day again, and although the sun shone brightly, it failed to disperse the ice in the puddles, or melt the frosted encrustations that resembled jewels on the grass beneath our feet. The summit plateau may have been bare and unassuming – in fact downright dull, but the view from the eastern edge of the escarpment was spacious and liberating and we chatted to a friendly Japanese gentleman who asked me to take his photograph with his own camera. I was quite envious of the advanced Japanese technology. In those days, there were few single lens reflex cameras available in Britain and those that were, such as the Leica, were far too expensive for an impecunious teenager. When we left the plateau to return to Barley, the transition from full daylight to the gloom of the evening was almost immediate. The descent by Pendle's eastern slopes was shaded from the setting sun by the bulk of the hill and many a light was shining in many a homestead before we were back in the hostel.

The following day was equally brilliant with frosted grass sparkling in the sun crunching delightfully beneath our feet, so rather than return by road all the way to Chatburn, we took the slanting path that crosses over Pendle's "Big End" from where we dropped down to meet the road above Downham. It was as well that the ground was frozen hard that day, for many times since then I have had mud over my ankles from using that route as a descent when Brenda has dropped me off in Barley and then driven round to meet me in Downham.

A World Above

He found the hill inside a tattered book.
Bewitched with romance, told his friend and took
her by the hand to climb a rocky path
that held no fears for those so much in love.

Struggling to rise above a world that tried
to hide beneath a shroud of mist, a thin
sun failed to pierce the shadowed, sleeping air.
Nor was there any sound except from feet
that crunched their imprints into frost rimmed grass
devoid of sheep. Seen from the summit cairn
and valley deep, a thousand pin-pricked lights
began to mirror stars while winter smoke
rose slow, untroubled, from a hundred hearths.
They drank the chilled white wine of happiness
before they had to turn, yet knowing they'd
go back, go back, go back. Until one day
in May he carried ashes in his pack.

Remembering places where they used to rest
he finds the stony climb seems steeper now.
The stream still chatters to itself each Spring
amongst the meadows bright with new-born lambs
in which she would delight. Each well-known step
he takes, she takes with him. But he will climb
the hill until one day he joins her there.

Pendle Hill's "Big End" seen from Ogden Clough reservoir
August 22nd 2009

Pendle Hill

Oh! Name of triple names my Pendle Hill.
Much less than mountain,
yet three times more than merely hill.
There, lapwing swooping ridges climb
the wind to skylark rippling
plover piping upland shadows racing
breathless over Spence and Mearley Moors.

Those moaning walls of gritstone barriers filter
dirges from the gale tossed ragged
grasses at their feet. At ease I greet
the distant ghostly curlew's gurgling call.
Inside your peat black cloughs, hag-ridden voices
bound in moss demand I sacrifice
on Beltane fires my love that burns for you.

Oh! Name of magic names my Pendle Hill,
cloud capped with hanging hail or hurricane,
or clothed in liquid winter sunshine, bridal white,
your witching name is branded on my heart.

OUTWARD BOUND

Note: The British Electricity Authority (BEA) changed its name in 1955 to Central Electricity Authority (CEA) and then again in 1956 to Central Electricity Generating Board (CEGB).

This essay, reproduced verbatim, was written in 1957 in response to a request by my employer, the Central Electricity Generating Board, (CEGB) to explain why I should be one of two trainees chosen from the North-west region to attend a 26 day course at the Outward Bound Mountain School (OBMS) based at Watermillock on Ullswater. Background information from the Outward Bound Trust (OBT) was included to help the applicants. I was already in thrall to the Lake District mountains and two years earlier I had spent a week Youth Hostelling there.

During my final year at school, I began to realise that education consisted of more than just chemical formulae and Latin verbs but was something intangible and of far wider application. In fact, education became for me a way of life, the art of living, and this is important since man cannot live alone, he is always a member of the family and state, and without education "Thou wilt become as nothing, a thing of no value".

Now the Outward Bound schools were formed to foster initiative and responsibility, to give boys a taste of action in tough conditions as a part of their education and "to provide a means of developing the capacity of these boys to face hazards, difficulties, hardships and emergencies of all kinds". At the heart of all these aims we perceive a common denominator in that they are all intended to improve a person's character, so contributing to his value, both as an individual and as a member of the community. The work of the Outward Bound Trust can also be extended to cover other facets of a person's character for instance when a boy is taken to a place far from the Hallsteads school and told to find his own way back, then his resourcefulness, endurance and courage are tested and improved.

While most of the above aims can be used by the individual to benefit the community, they are mainly to the advantage of the individual himself. But the O.B.M.S. also gives training in teamwork and strives to show that the team spirit of a person is only proportional to the amount of effort put into the communal work in question. The value of these aims is self-evident and being an active Youth Club worker, I feel that, given the opportunity to increase the scope of my education by attending an Outward Bound course, I could more worthily fulfil my obligations in this field. Education then, does not even consist only in the accumulation of knowledge however broad the scope, but can be extended to practical and spiritual help given to those in need.

In these days of dreary television, of rock n' roll, sobbing crooners and the like, it is encouraging to have the chance to attend such a course, indeed, living as I do in an industrial area, it would be delightful to leave the squalid, smoke-ridden atmosphere of Wigan and spend 26 days breathing the sparkling fresh air of the Lake District.

The fundamental aims of the O.B.T. are admirably summed up in the words of its motto: "To serve, to strive and not to yield" where the ends in view are to develop self-reliance and self-confidence, and to bring to the surface a knowledge of one's inner resources, spiritually, mentally and physically. There surely could be no better motto, nor can a man do more than serve his fellows to the utmost, forever strive for their well-being and with whatever he is faced, never to yield.

My essay had clearly been much appreciated by Mr Parker, head of the CEGB education and training section because I was selected to attend the 22nd course to be held at Hallsteads, a large house on the shore of Ullswater at Watermillock. The course began on

55

August 26th 1957 but before then Brenda and I had become engaged, and I had arranged another Lake District tour with her in place of my cousin John. Of such is the fickle nature of friendship, although John (I think) understood my reasons because over 60 years later we are still the best of friends.

A SECOND LAKE DISTRICT CIRCUIT (2)

Unlike the previous anti-clockwise circuit recorded above, this time I decided on a clockwise route but again starting from Windermere, and since Brenda's father was a railway traffic controller based at Liverpool Lime Street, Brenda was entitled to a rail travel concession. That may explain why we went to the Lake District by rail from Wigan, although we had to change trains at Oxenholme. We were early enough in Windermere with enough time to ascend Orrest Head as I'd done with John two years earlier and again the weather was glorious. We both carried well used rucksacks but were both young and fit enough to return to the town and wander down to Bowness and take the ferry across the lake to the Ferry House without hurrying. In any case it was too hot to hurry. From there, we followed the road through Sawrey, past Beatrix Potter's old home, Hill Top, to the charming hostel in Hawkshead for our first night.

At that time, Alfred Wainwright was largely unknown; he had published The Eastern Fells in 1955 and The Far Eastern Fells in 1956 and I had only become aware of his masterful handiwork from a single article (and sketch) in the Lancashire Evening Post. I thought then how talented he must be and gradually acquired a full set of his guides to the Lakeland fells, but he had yet to cover most of my planned route. I was using a recently bought one inch Ordnance Survey Lake District Tourist map, which incidentally, I consider to be a cartographic masterpiece, and I would happily have had one framed and hung on my bedroom wall. It is still popular and often found exhibited in many hotels and guest houses in the area and beyond.

We left Hawkshead the next morning to climb out of the village by the road heading for Coniston and intended to take in Tarn Hows *en route* but were overtaken by a Land Rover driven by a Millom scoutmaster who offered us a lift which we readily accepted – it was hot work climbing in the heat of the morning. I had my map out and was looking for a suitable spot to be dropped off as close as possible to Tarn Hows at the top of a hill. Absent-mindedly I left it behind when he left us. He would no doubt find it when he reached his own destination and maybe worry about his passengers who had kindly donated their valuable map to him. I bought a replacement anyway in Coniston, at the same time cursing my own forgetfulness. We would certainly need it in the days to come.

The real walking began after a day of rest exploring the gorge at Tilberthwaite that was once criss-crossed by several bridges. It became a very popular excursion for Victorian tourists. As we ascended the gorge, we came across traces of the bridges which were then derelict and clearly unsafe to use, so we had to scramble out of the gorge until we came to a point where we could climb down to rest in the sun. On such a day it was a real pleasure to remove our boots and bathe our feet in the deliciously cool waters of Tilberthwaite Gill. We saw nobody at all while we were there and returned to Coniston Far End hostel by way of the Yewdale Fell path.

We were due to spend the next night in Eskdale so we had a long day ahead and set off early. By 11.00 am we had reached the top of the Walna Scar track with the sun high in the sky and were soon down in the Duddon Valley where I remember noticing that the tar was boiling as we walked along a short stretch of road in search of a River Duddon crossing, marked on the map as "stepping-stones". From the far bank, we climbed the hillside to pass by the farm buildings at Grassguards, but we still had Birker Moor to cross, but without any definite path. Very soon, we seemed to be lost in an endless wasteland of waist high bracken, accompanied by a million flies. Eventually we began to descend to the River Esk and with burning feet on the Eskdale road and the glorious shade of some occasional trees we were soon at the long remembered youth hostel and its divine cold showers.

The next day I'd intended an ascent of Scafell Pike, but the heat wave continued and after the toil of the previous day neither of us relished the prospect of more such exertion. Instead, we took a ride on La'al Ratty, the miniature railway once used to carry iron ore to the coast from Dalegarth to Ravenglass. There we bought a newspaper and tried to find somewhere out of the sun to cool down.

For our next hostel I'd booked three nights at Black Sail hut. Until then we had not climbed a single mountain, but I had planned a couple of excursions from the hut that would soon rectify that. The only drawback was that to get there we had to cross two passes with concomitant climbs. We left Eskdale by climbing up the path that begins close to the Woolpack Inn and crossed Burnmoor to have lunch by Lingmell Beck where two well-meaning elderly ladies, for whom we had opened a gate, told us that an excellent lunch could be had at the Wasdale Head Hotel (as if two teenagers could afford such luxury). It was a sore trial climbing to the top of Black Sail Pass in the heat of the afternoon. I have memories of an intense heat, of unending moorland, and a relentless slog relieved only by a single halt by a stream where water splashing on to the rocks dispersed with a hiss of steam. We couldn't find a cool, let alone a cold place to sit and I swear we could have fried an egg on rocks that seemed to glow with an inner heat.

We had a well-earned rest at the top of the pass looking down to the Forestry Commission plantings that so disfigured the wild beauty of Ennerdale at that time. We descended into the cool depths of paradise and were two of only three hostellers there for the first night. Sunlight was flooding the dormitory through the door when I woke the next morning. I'd left the door open all night again on account of the heat but unlike my previous visit, this time we were not joined by a weary sheep. But I did begin to wonder if it were always so hot at Black Sail hut, although I don't like to imagine how it must be when rain beats up the valley and a gale force wind howls around its substantial walls.

For our first full day there, we retraced our steps to the top of Black Sail pass from where we turned left to make a direct ascent of Kirk Fell. Brenda wasn't too keen but heroically submitted to my assurances that we wouldn't need to return that way. I'm sure now that she never revealed to me her real feelings but would subsequently allow me to indulge what she must have guessed was my insatiable love of wild places. Eventually, as you will see, she was content to let me go off on my own while she would find enough to occupy herself at sea level. From Kirk Fell we continued to Beckhead and thence by Moses' Trod, the old pony track that traverses the fell-side below the impressive Northern crags of Great Gable. From Windy Gap we took the short climb to the top of Green Gable, where we rested to watch the shadows lengthen as the sun began its long, slow descent beyond Pillar, before we did the same ourselves and were back at the hostel in time for supper.

Black Sail dormitory open door
July 1957

We slept well that night and woke to find Great Gable wrapped in a blanket of cloud. I washed early (and perhaps foolishly) in the nearby stream, but didn't need treatment for frostbite. There was a cold wind blowing up the valley, so we wrapped up warmly to climb Pillar by returning up to the pass, but this time turned right at the top to find a refuge for lunch on the summit out of the biting wind. Pillar is far removed from the major tourist routes that cluster round the centre of the Lake District, so I didn't expect to come across many people up there and I was right – we saw nobody all day, even on a July Saturday. The wind eased off after lunch and it was a pleasure to get rid of our outer wind protection and enjoy the warmth of the sun as we took in the distant view under yet another cloudless sky. The well-known view of the Scafells was barely visible through a heat haze, but looking to the north and west, the views of the hills of Galloway across the Solway, and of the Isle of Man were glorious.

Perhaps we dozed off then because it was late afternoon before we began to descend by way of Wind Gap and High Beck through a trackless hollow that in my imagination resembled a typical Scottish corrie, known to me then only from photographs. All the while, I was scanning the forest below that extended all the way down the valley to Gillerthwaite looking for a way through what appeared to be impenetrable trees, hoping there might be a bridge across the River Liza. It would be a long trek if there wasn't, and possibly a blazing row or a trudge back in sullen silence. But fortunately, we came across a fire break which we followed for a while, threading our way through conifers that obscured any distant view, to a clearly recently constructed bridge. I breathed a sigh of relief that Brenda never heard.

We had an easy day after that, crossing the fells to Honister and the hostel at Rosthwaite in Borrowdale. The heat wave continued and we bought a newspaper (The Guardian) and bread at Rosthwaite post office. The newspaper would be useful later in the day. We walked over to Watendlath, explored the tiny hamlet and then took the road north towards Ashness Woods. We left the road for a while for no other reason than to sleep half the afternoon away on the bracken clad hillside, disturbed only by rumbles of thunder echoing

61

from crag to crag. It was far too hot and humid for strenuous climbing. We descended then by Lodore Falls but these were a great disappointment for there had been no rain for many days. But I was to learn one more salutary lesson. Being by then accustomed to so many hot and sunny days, we had set off without waterproofs. I should have heeded the thunder and set off back much earlier.

As we approached the Bowder Stone, the inevitable happened and the long overdue break in the weather began, at first only a few drops, but these soon became a gentle shower and we ran to the famous rock for shelter which we shared, along with many others, beneath its massive overhanging roofs. We were lucky to be there before the heavens opened with an unmatched ferocity. As soon as we considered the rain had slackened enough, we set off back to the hostel with Brenda trying as best she could to keep her hair dry (rather unsuccessfully) using the Manchester Guardian.

The Bowder Stone
August 10th 2007

62

Summer Heat

On Orrest Head against the saw-toothed
Western sky I photographed you in your
    chequered shirt and denim jeans.
I longed for more than being merely friends.
    We found, before Millennium crowds,
    the secret paths of Tilberthwaite and lay
    by quiet pools beneath that burning
summer sky where only sheep would watch.
    By Walna Scar we crossed the hills
    and rode the toast-racked baby train
        to Ravenglass. And still the sun
    burnt down. More hills by frazzled
    becks to Black Sail Hut. Cold washing
in the infant stream. We lay again by toasted
rocks above the road to Ashness Bridge while
        rolling thunder crashed across
    Watendlath`s sky and refuge found
    beneath a shivering Bowder Stone.

    Then showered in separate rooms,
        courtesy of the YHA.

I had planned our next hostel to be at Patterdale. This had
required a careful study of several time-tables so we used three
buses and a lake steamer. That is to say, we took the bus from
Rosthwaite to Keswick, from Keswick to Penrith, from Penrith to
Pooley Bridge and from there sailed on the Lady of the Lake (I
think it was) to Glenridding with only a mile left to walk to the
hostel. Despite the rains of the previous day, there was insufficient
water at the hostel for washing so it was back to washing in the
stream and using a chemical toilet. How times have changed!
    Brenda had already experienced the exposure of Crib Goch's
narrow ridge so I had no worries about taking her over Striding
Edge and we had a splendid walk without any difficulty. We had

left our rucksacks at the hostel and, as the forecast was for a calm day, we carried only the bare necessities such as food, drink and medical supplies, but Helvellyn's summit was not a place to linger. I've no recollection of the state of the summit when I was there with John but on that day it was a disgusting expanse of litter. Papers, plastic bottles, tin cans and every other kind of detritus that humans throw away despoiled the summit shelter. We didn't stay and turned south over Nethermost Pike and Dollywagon Pike to drop down to Grizedale Tarn and the Brothers' Parting where Wordsworth said farewell to his brother John, not knowing he would never see him again.

That was effectively the last day of our holiday. I had a gastric upset the next day that persisted until after we'd returned home two days later by train from Keswick. We had walked by road from Patterdale to Dockray from where we caught the Penrith to Keswick bus. In Keswick, I couldn't resist visiting the museum and playing *Crimond*, the hymn tune usually used for *The Lord's My Shepherd*, on the musical stones exhibited there.

Back at work I learned that my essay for the Outward Bound Trust had done enough to secure a place for me on the course that would begin that August. I would soon be back amongst my beloved hills, the only drawback being that I would need to abstain from alcohol and cigarettes for twenty six consecutive days.

U 22

Not as you might think a German submarine but the name of the course I attended at the Ullswater Outward Bound School (OBMS) in August 1957. I was, I think, the oldest "teenager" there but had only recently discarded that appellation. I may also have been the most experienced. There were ninety-six of us and we were soon learning about abseiling, mountain rescue, first aid, field cooking and the intricacies of map-reading. We were divided into eight "patrols", each of twelve boys with a specified instructor who arbitrarily chose a leader for his patrol from among us that would last for the twenty six days of the course.

Ullswater Outward Bound Mountain School
1957

The Warden then was Major Geoffrey Douglas who was assisted by eight instructors. He ran the school with a strict discipline based on what I suppose now was a hangover from his army days. Smoking and alcohol were of course forbidden, as was consorting with any one of the young girls who did the cooking.

Every day without exception we were required to take an early morning dip (naked) in Ullswater, so we had to congregate at 6.30 am, with one or two instructors in control, beneath the canopy in the school yard before we jogged a quarter of a mile to the lake. At that time of day dawn was just about breaking and there were bats flying about which disturbed the more timorous amongst us. But, for fear of being humiliated, nobody dared miss the ritual, even on the three days when we set off on excursions away from the school and the time was brought forward to 6.00 am.

*The yard where we gathered
before running to jump or dive into Ullswater
September 1957*

We were there for three days before we had our first excursion carrying full packs into the fells to climb The Knott and Thornthwaite Crag, two minor summits that I remembered from my circuit with my cousin John in 1955. On Thornthwaite Crag we ate lunch and chatted with Mr Crowther, our instructor, each of us adding our own contribution to the conversation, but I soon became bored. I'd been there before and could name all the distant peaks that Mr. Crowther pointed to. Maybe I wasn't listening and should have paid more attention to my leader, but when I looked up from studying my map, lost in my own world, I realised that I was alone. The whole party had upped and gone! Fortunately, we'd been told where we were to spend the night, so I set off alone to follow the path towards the Kirkstone Pass over Stony Cove Pike (Caudale Moor for Wainwright followers) and soon met one of our party sent back to search for me. I was only missing for about fifteen minutes and wasn't at all worried, but I can only imagine what Mr Crowther must have been thinking. Whether or not he reported the incident I don't know, nor whether it was he or I that was at fault. We camped that night by the Kirkstone road in a walled field below Red Screes.

The next day we experienced thick mist through which Mr Crowther, led us unerringly over Little Hart Crag, Dove Crag and Hart Crag to the summit of Fairfield. I noted in my log-book (that we were all expected to keep) that I wouldn't have been too happy to have been in charge under those conditions. I was impressed by the orienteering skill of Mr Crowther, and also to the attention to safety taken by the OBMS which only served to heighten the sense of irresponsibility of the (then) BEA on our expedition to Coniston Old Man three years earlier. On our second night we camped by Brownrigg Well, a spring not far from the summit of Helvellyn. We were unfortunate the next morning that there was no visible sunrise and were split into groups of four to return to the school. Mist had cloaked the plateau as we ate breakfast, but I decided to take my group down by Swirral Edge and I was much gratified that out of 24 groups we were the second group back at the school. Several groups had apparently mistaken Thirlmere for Ullswater.

The following days included cross country practice, athletics, first aid, canoeing, rock climbing, knotting, forestry and abseiling. Another excursion required us to walk, again with full packs, to Hollows Farm at Grange in Borrowdale so we followed the old coach road from Dockray to St. John's Vale accompanied by magnificent views of Blencathra whose impressive ridges had me wishing all the time to be up there. We continued over Walla Crag and descended into Borrowdale by the side of Cat Gill. The next day we were expected to walk alone along a pre-set route (no doubt being observed from a distance) taking in Rosthwaite, Rigg Head quarries, Honister Pass, Seatoller, Watendlath and Lodore Falls. I have an idea that we were supposed to use the road, but I ignored the voice of authority and cut off a corner to take the old road to the top of Honister Pass against a strong headwind. Approaching the top of the pass, the heavens opened and soaked me for the first time that day. I made a fast descent to Seatoller and Rosthwaite and I was dry by the time I reached Watendlath from where I continued to Ashness woods and returned to Grange by following the true left bank of Lodore Falls where considerably more water was cascading down than I had seen earlier in the year with Brenda.

Later, our patrol was taken up Kings How by way of the path through the little Troutdale side valley, to be dropped off at intervals to spend the night alone fending for ourselves. I was one of the last to be left alone not far from the top, Others discovered some caves much lower down where they were lucky enough to spend the night sharing the space with friends, but I was abandoned in the midst of an almost barren hillside. It didn't take me long though, to find a convenient rock large enough for me to use as a windshield and bivouac. A nearby holly tree growing from a vertical crag had roots that concealed a mass of surprisingly dry sticks and branches on such a wet day. Castle Crag, lower down across the valley, was frequently blotted out by driving rain that swept up the hillside, but I managed to prepare a dish of hot tomato soup.

O.K. it wasn't hot, but it was warm enough and I wouldn't suffer from hunger during the night. I'd taken dry clothes and changed beneath my bivvy sheet without getting too wet and even succeeded in sleeping for a while. I remember distinctly my frozen fingers struggling with obstinate buttons, my feet and head protruding from opposite ends of my tiny half tent, the rock that served as a pillow and the wind that blew straight through. However, I have a positive memory that I did sleep because at one point I woke thinking that it was daylight, only to see a brilliant moon riding high on storm swept clouds.

Morning arrived with storm clouds still scudding across the sky, so I abandoned all thoughts of a cooked breakfast until I was back at base. Being independent and a little rebellious, I wanted to do a little exploring on my own and spurned the path by which I'd been taken up in favour of the Watendlath path to Rosthwaite where I crossed the Derwent to climb Castle Crag. It was too good an opportunity to miss. Of course, I then had to skirt round the camp site in order to arrive from the correct direction. Life once again became a luxury as many sleeping bags were hung on trees to dry in the wind before a huge fire and the day given over to gossip and what each of us had done in the night. That was when I learned that many of my companions had spent the night comfortably in dry caves below Grange Fell. That night we pitied those who had followed in our footsteps as thunderclaps resounded and echoed across the valley and lightning rent the darkened skies.

The next day, on wet rocks we practised our rock climbing skills on Brown Slabs, part of Shepherds Crag, as more rain swept across the valley. For the record my climbs were The Arete, The Direct and The Introductory. In later years I would return to Brown Slabs to climb with my daughter Kathryn, and later lead my younger brother, Peter, up Little Chamonix.

Back at the school the instructors had organised a cross country run that included a number of check points and also took in the summit of Gowbarrow Fell. Approaching the summit I diverged from the path that all those in front of me were using and cut across a corner of the fell through waist high bracken, so gaining several places. This action was, of course, observed and later that I day I was reprimanded for "taking unfair advantage" but when I argued that nobody had told us to follow a set route and I had used my initiative, I was commended but, I think ruefully. The course ended with a third course in which groups of four were expected to take three days to walk to Scafell Pike and back carrying all their food, tents and sleeping bags. This was clearly intended to test everything we had been taught over the preceding three weeks. The one incident that remains to be told is the subject of the next chapter. The rest of the course was an anti-climax.

ACCIDENTS WILL HAPPEN (1)

My longest abiding memory of U22 is of the third and final expedition which we did in groups of four without guidance from our instructors. Our orders were to visit Scafell Pike and return to the school on the third day after visiting a number of pre-arranged checkpoints. Some were sent by way of Langdale and others through Grasmere. We were to visit Helvellyn's summit. We set off in high spirits knowing that we would soon be returning home and that our standard of fitness was high enough to carry us through safely. Rain began at Glenridding, a thin, all pervading drizzle that eventually turned into a heavy downpour that continued unabated for the next 36 hours.

We reached Helvellyn by way of Red Tarn and Swirral Edge with hardly a halt to find an Elastoplast tin at the summit shelter in which to record our passing. We were the first group through. We were checked by our instructors at Dunmail Raise before we were allowed to continue to Greenup Edge via Wythburn. In gathering gloom, cloud and incessant rain we plodded on, contouring around Raise to gain the top of the Stake Pass with Borrowdale and Eagle Crag observed mistily below us. Somewhere thereabouts I stumbled on a grassy tussock and fell heavily, sustaining a very painful sprain to my left ankle. For me, the rest of the expedition was one long hell! However, I struggled on until we pitched our tents for the night by Angle Tarn where we could summon up only enough energy to provide ourselves with hot cocoa while the rain continued to fall. At least we changed into dry clothing for a reasonable night's sleep.

We woke to find rain still falling and the wind literally roaring up from Borrowdale. We ate and dressed hurriedly and thought it best to be on our way as soon as possible and away from that god-forsaken spot. At Esk Hause we found George Fisher's (he of the well-known Keswick mountain clothing and equipment shop) tent abandoned and a note explaining that he had "…rescued a half drowned woman from Grains Gill and had perforce taken her to shelter." I loved that sentence so much that for a while I forgot the pain that consumed my ankle because it told me so much about

George. He was, as you might expect, a member of the Keswick Mountain rescue team and would naturally go to the aid of someone in need rather than merely wait in his tent to meet a series of youngsters passing by who could all take care of themselves. It was also his use of the word *perforce* which is a wonderful short-hand word that tells so much and was so suited to that occasion.

We continued then until we reached a pile of broken rocks that seemed to tower above us. I didn't know then that we had reached Broad Crag, so confusing was the mist. At that point the others began looking to me for advice – they knew that I had climbed Scafell Pike before. So here I quote verbatim from a note I made at the time: *At this point the path dipped sharply into impenetrable mist and in our condition we decided not to continue since by now the wind was mighty and the rain and mist were soaking us through – as if not already. With my ankle giving me pain at every step, I doubt that further progress was possible.*

And now for a sober analysis (written in retrospect in 1963). Was our decision to turn back correct? I have the meagre satisfaction of knowing that no other group reached Scafell Pike that day because they were all deliberately turned back at Esk Hause by our instructors, (my group had passed through too soon). The facts are these:

1. We were tired and weary, having walked 18 miles and climbed 5,000 ft carrying 40lb loads the previous day.
2. We had spent the previous night cold, wet and miserable under canvas in incessant rain and wind at 2,500 ft and had eaten little (although probably enough).
3. Two years had passed since I was last on Scafell Pike and had then approached the summit from the Corridor Route (before Wainwright). My memory was not good enough to recognise the summit under the prevailing conditions so there was some doubt as to where we were.
4. I had a badly twisted, if not sprained ankle.
5. The weather was even then deteriorating and was already worse than anything I had ever come across – and I was the most experienced member of our group.

6. We took two hours to cover the two miles from Esk Hause to Broad Crag and back.
7. It had been instilled into us that, like Shackleton and Scott, we should never give up!

The fact that subsequent groups were not allowed to attempt the final leg to Scafell Pike suggests to me that our decision was correct. My feelings at the time were that if we had continued, then the OBMS would have been reporting one group missing (presumed dead?) Of course that would not have happened for we had our tents, but I will never forget the path that seemed to jump over the rocky declivities of Broad Crag to drop apparently vertically into the swirling mists far below. In fact it was barely possible to stand, let alone climb down with our packs into that witches' cauldron. The last line of this episode is the one line from my end of course report which states: "Mountain Craft – Honours".

Ingleborough 6.00 am

As dawn distils tip-toeing sunrise into day
I stumble on the rattling, chattering stones
that bouncing down the mountain path
awake the phantom guards that
bleating lurch away
reluctantly on frost stained turf.
Higher still across the plain
the crimson king
confronts me rising from the
eastern depths of his domain.
His breath dissolves
the mist. Unlocks
the mystery, paints colours
on the plateau's parchment
staining red the grey bones of a distant past.

EARLY RECOLLECTIONS

Our interests, character and relationships with others develop as we age, so it's reasonable to suppose that while young, the genes we are born with are the first major influences on our behaviour. Experience will come in time and nature versus nurture is a subject that will be discussed as long as babies continue to be born. However, as we grow older, we are moulded and changed, not only in appearance but also by how we perceive our place in society.

Brenda completed her studies to become a State Registered Nurse in 1959 and was awarded the gold medal for her year. The hospital authorities were hoping then to employ her as a tutor but we were in love and "truly, madly, deeply" doesn't come anywhere near, so we were married soon afterwards in April of that year. We'd already had some differences of opinion during our courting days, so we knew a lot about each other's interests and temperament and Brenda was already aware of my addiction to, and love of hills, mountains and wild places. After all, she had accompanied me on many excursions; some of which have been related above. Although she never spoke of it, I now suspect that she may have thought, as Diana, Princess of Wales so eloquently expressed it – "there were three of us in that marriage."

We spent our honeymoon in Borrowdale at the Borrowdale Hotel which was probably my choice owing to the bus stop at the front door which guaranteed that a variety of walks and climbs would be within easy access. During the week we climbed Castle Crag where we encountered the Blencathra hounds in full pursuit of a fox running down from Maiden Moor. On another day we climbed Grange Fell from Troutdale to look for the site where I spent my OBMS bivouac site two years previously. Close to the summit we came across a newly born ailing lamb with no mother in sight. The nearest farm was at Rosthwaite but we were told that the lamb would have been dropped from a sheep belonging to a farm in Watendlath so we retraced most of our walk only to be horrified when the farmer thanked us and said he would put it in the oven. Seeing our apparent horror, he explained it had probably been born prematurely, had been deserted by its mother and would be suffering from hypothermia. It needed to be warmed up.

Grange Fell

Nothing was moving save the grass
stirred by the wind sweeping clean
the fellside bearing the sad bleating.
We came first on the afterbirth
muddying the ground, glistening.

Then the lone lamb, cold and slippery
calling vainly, deserted, motherless,
potential carrion. Crow black
undertakers squabbled for a
piece of the action but you gently
lifted the ragged lump of woollen waste
and I carried the plastic waterproof
mackintosh wrapped bundle down to
Watendlath where a nonchalant farmer
thrust it into the oven's warmth.
Too weak to stand, abandoned by
its mother, it might survive.

By then our day was lost. Our
plans awry. But your nursing instinct,
love and skill, had saved a life.

I wanted to revisit the OBMS school on Ullswater to show Brenda where I'd been two years earlier, but that wasn't easy. We needed to take two buses to reach Penruddock on the A66 and then had a five mile walk there and back to the school on Ullswater. Although we arrived without an appointment, we were well received and were treated to tea and biscuits. I remembered some of the patrol leaders, although the Warden, Major Douglas, had left, possibly because, while I'd been there on U22, he was planning a trip to the Himalaya with a well-known climber, Hamish MacInnes, to search, so we understood, for the yeti. The floor of one room at the school had then been completely covered with all the equipment that they would need. Major Douglas had been succeeded by Squadron Leader Lester Davis F.R.G.S.

On another day, we took the bus from the front door of the hotel to Seatoller and climbed Great Gable via Styhead on a day of intermittent sleet and rain. It wasn't the most enjoyable day because we only had plastic macs to serve as wet weather clothing. Not surprisingly we didn't linger on the summit.

By August, Brenda was pregnant, but we were both ready for another holiday. For the August Bank Holiday we decided on Great Langdale and stupidly went without booking (or thinking) ahead. We, (that is, I) had a romantic desire to stay at the Old Dungeon Ghyll (ODG) hotel. I knew the hotel had a long history and had been a favourite haunt for many famous rock climbers, so we took the bus to the head of the valley. Of course, I should have known that the hotel would be full, as were the New Dungeon Ghyll Hotel and every other hostelry on the walk back to Elterwater where at last we found a guest house offering B & B with a vacant room.

Brenda never complained although it had been a very hot and thirsty walk. An elderly couple who owned a car were also staying there and kindly took us to an organ concert in Grasmere Church that evening. They also accompanied us the next day when we climbed the Langdale Pikes, though Brenda was content to rest below Loft Crag rather than complete the walk. But she must have sensed that I was yearning for something more adventurous, because she said that if I wanted a day amongst the hills, she would spend the day in Ambleside.

Bank Holiday

Imperceptibly, like ripening fruit
you swelled. The miracle was,
we went to Langdale unbooked
on August Bank Holiday without a car.
From the Old Dungeon Ghyll it was
a long walk back, no vacancies
until Elterwater. But we were young
and would survive. Especially you,
who knew I had, and have, another
love. And so we climbed the Langdales
three of us, you and I and our unborn girl.
In Grasmere church
poetry and music, courtesy
of the fearless Corlesses who bravely drove
their Sunbeam Talbot over Red Bank.
But there was little traffic then.

How could I dare to leave you both
in Ambleside while I on Crinkle Crags
explored a higher world?

I took the bus up the valley and walked the length of Mickleden
from the ODG to climb by Rossett Gill to Angle Tarn from where
the north facing slopes of Hanging Knotts on Bowfell were too
enticing to miss. There's no recognised path that way but the
steepness attracted me and seen from below there seemed to be
enough grassy ledges between a series of small, exposed crags to
make a direct line possible.

I was right and had no trouble going where few people, if any,
had ever been, although I recorded in my diary that it had been an
exciting climb. From the summit of Bowfell I continued over
Crinkle Crags noticing in front of me one other lone walker. I was
catching up with him but despite the short distance that he was

ahead of me, by the time I reached the spot he had disappeared – an easy thing to do on the twisting craggy outcrops of the Crinkle ridge. The circumstances were such that I imagined then that it must be the elusive Mr Wainwright, who was already renowned for his dislike of company, but I didn't hang about in search of whoever it was. I ran down a gully by Crinkle Gill and arrived at the ODG in glorious sunlight for a glass of cider. It was very cloudy so could have been from the bottom of the barrel, but I was so thirsty I wasn't going to complain. It was delicious and I suffered no ill effects.

Before our second wedding anniversary we had two girls – Rosalind, who ascended Cat Bells aged six months in a baby carrier, and Kathryn, who would later walk up Gummers How aged three. Brenda insisted, and always ensured, that every year we would have at least one good holiday in addition to days out and Bank Holiday weekends, so in August 1960, we booked a double room (with a cot for Rosalind) for a week at the Lake Hotel in Keswick, advertised then as being "Nearest the Lake". We had no car, so we travelled to Keswick by rail, changing at Penrith. Brenda was pregnant with Kathryn at the time, and we had taken the pram so we could walk easily to the Castlerigg Stone Circle and do other low level walks. I took Brenda and Rosalind, who was in a baby carrier slung round my neck, over Walla Crag but on Cat Bells, Brenda preferred to rest half-way up rather than climb to the top.

The Keswick Motor Company premises were then on Lake Road directly opposite the hotel, so it was easy to arrange a day trip by coach to the Western lakes, an area new to me at that time. We were taken as far as possible towards the bottom of Honister Pass and may have been taken through Whinlatter Forest but I'm not sure about that. Beyond Gatesgarth there was an area where the driver could turn the coach round for the return journey. There he allowed his passengers to leave the coach and stretch their legs before returning along the shores of Buttermere, Crummock Water and Loweswater.

Brenda holding Rosalind beside a Bedford Super Vega coach (based at Keswick), at Gatescarth below Honister August 19th 1960

Brenda, however, could tell I was pining for something adventurous to climb, so one rainy day she suggested I go off on my own. I told her I would climb the Scafells after taking the bus to Seatoller. Suspecting that she might be alarmed and forbid me going, I didn't mention that I hoped to climb Cust's Gully on Great End. This is a serious climb under snow and ice in winter, but a reasonably easy rock climb in summer and might just have been within my ability to climb it safely alone. I had no trouble locating the gully by means of the enormous chockstone that bridges it high up but, having climbed into the gully, I found it was so wet and slimy that I abandoned the idea as too dangerous to attempt under the circumstances.

I still intended to take the direct route from Scafell Pike to Scafell by way of Mickledore and Broad Stand though – another easy rock climb and one up which I would lead Rosalind years later. On that day, the rocks were wet and slippery, and I spent quite some time on what was clearly going to be a hard move on the left side of what I recall as being a vertical wall. From my reading, I knew that there would be nothing to worry me above that point. I had no rope or other safety aids, so I was very careful about my balance and contact with the rock. But I was wearing vibram soled boots and when one foot slipped from its foothold I was left hanging by one hand with empty space below me and the potential of a fatal fall threatening.

I lowered myself down gently to the ledge from which I'd climbed a moment earlier and, with a rapidly beating heart, took stock of the situation. The problem was obviously the wet rock and the rubber soles of my boots, so I removed the boots, tied the laces together and hung the boots round my neck. My stocking clad feet gave me a perfect grip and seconds later I was on the easier, safer ground above. I greatly enjoyed the rest of the day, but that incident taught me much about myself and my responsibilities as a husband and father – and I haven't forgotten.

A year later, now with two children under two years of age we had an early week in a Llandudno hotel that provided a baby-sitting service. This was a welcome release for Brenda from the constant need to care for the children. Although I did as much as I could to help, she had to care for them all day every day. She was missing the chance to use her nursing skills and about that time began to work one night a week at our local hospital.

In August 1961, we made a compromise – I would take Brenda's brother, David and my brother Peter, for a week of youth hostelling in the Lake District. During the week, my mum and dad would bring her and the children to see us and stay for two nights at the Rothay Hotel in Grasmere. By then, we had acquired a soft top, three-wheeled Reliant Regal, a cousin of the famous Reliant Robin (of Fools and Horses fame), the only car we could afford that could be driven legally on a motorcycle driving licence.

I drove it to Coniston and left it at Hellen's garage for the week. The first day we walked from Coniston Far End Y.H. by way of the Old Man, Brim Fell, Swirl How, Great Carrs (where we passed some aircraft wreckage) to Grey Friar without incident and descended to the adopted youth hostel at Troutal. The next day we crossed the River Duddon by Birks Bridge and I led the boys to the top of Harter Fell for my first distant view of the grandeur of upper Eskdale. I think it must surely be the finest view in the whole Lake District from a summit which is itself one of the finest. We had an easy descent to Eskdale and rested in front of the hostel after our evening meal watching the shadows lengthen across the valley. The far side was bathed in a softness of evening light that I have still not found anywhere else in the world – and believe me, I have travelled.

The following day I took the boys round the head of Eskdale hoping to include the summits of Crinkle Crags, Bowfell, Esk Pike, Ill Crag, Broad Crag, Scafell Pike and Scafell. It was a long day, taking ten hours, and we returned to the hostel just as the dinner gong was sounding – and I'd had to omit Scafell. The next day, David had an easy day riding on La'al Ratty to Ravenglass while I took Peter to the deliciously rocky top of Slight Side following one of the many routes to the top of Scafell. Slight Side itself is seldom visited except by climbers wishing to complete the list of Mr Wainwright's summits. In fact, Scafell itself is much less popular than Scafell Pike, the latter being the highest point in England. So not surprisingly we met nobody until we were back on the road in Eskdale.

Peter on top of Slight Side. Harter Fell in the distance
August 1961

After three nights in Eskdale we were due to meet the rest of the family to share a picnic at Cockley Beck in the Duddon valley at the foot of Hard Knott pass. This was an opportunity to introduce David and Peter to the Roman Fort that lies to the left of the motor road about half-way up the pass on the Eskdale side. Once we'd had a wander round to identify the Commandant's house and sundry other buildings, I took Peter up Hardknott Fell by way of the Roman parade ground that lies above the fort. David stayed behind to wait for our return. We had an enjoyable reunion with the family before mum and dad returned with Brenda and our girls back to Grasmere while I walked with David and Peter down the Duddon Valley for another night at Troutal Y.H.. Our last day saw us walking back over Walna Scar to pick up the car in Coniston.

I remember many first ascents, by which I don't mean the first ascent by someone else, but your first ascent of a summit or crag where you've never been. There's always something special about such days, perhaps a sense that you're exploring new territory and you don't know what to expect, even though you may have read as much as you can about it. One such day was in March 1964, when I left Brenda at home caring for the girls and I took my brother Peter, then aged fourteen to climb the North-west ridge of Catstycam – the Helvellyn outlier at the end of Swirral Edge. Snow was still lying, though not so much as to be dangerous if we took care. The M6 north of Broughton had been opened recently so we were at Glenridding in under two hours. The ridge looks impossible seen from Raise owing to foreshortening but it rises as straight as the flight of an arrow to a delightful tiny peak.

There was cloud about when we left the car but as we climbed into Keppel Cove, the sun appeared and the whole mountainside began to steam as if from the heat of a subterranean fire. We climbed straight into the eye of the sun and had to loosen our clothing as we grew hotter and hotter. I was not as fit as I thought, and Peter would frequently pull away and then need to wait for me to catch up. We climbed steadily through a slight haze, sufficient to spread the glare of the sun reflected from patches of snow, but not so thick as to obscure the distant view of Ullswater. Suddenly, about 50 yards ahead of me, Peter gave a triumphant shout – he had reached the summit, a splendid place of smooth, short-cropped grass and sun-warmed rocks from which enticing slopes dropped away on all sides. We had to kick steps in the snows of Swirral Edge and climbed into mist for the last couple of hundred feet to Helvellyn where we came across crisp frozen snow and an abrupt fall in temperature.

Another memorable first for me was the ascent of Jack's Rake on Pavey Ark a month later, again with Peter. We began the climb in mist that became thicker the further we climbed until we reached Stickle Tarn. Nobody else was there and not even the gentle breeze that ruffled the surface of Stickle Tarn disturbed the eerie silence. The scene was redolent of Arthurian legends. I would not have been surprised if a hand clutching Excalibur had risen from the lake. As we rested by the shore, the mist began to disperse revealing the topmost crags of Pavey Ark. Gradually the whole crag became visible as the sun came out in its full glory and the ascent became a climb of pure unbounded pleasure. Any danger that might arise from the steepness of Jack's Rake is to some extent mitigated by the security of its retaining wall (effectively a craggy irregular banister). The deep blue sky patterned with clouds racing across from somewhere behind the rocks above lent a kind of magic to the beauty of the climb.

All too soon we were negotiating the tricky exposed slabs at the top where the route becomes indistinct and it's possible that we actually climbed the final chimney of Great Gully. I'd planned it to be an easy day so we ambled over to Thunacar Knott, had lunch on Harrison Stickle, visited Loft Crag and Pike o' Stickle and finished the day by scrambling around the lower rocks of Gimmer Crag.

Brenda and I returned to Eskdale in October 1969, taking Brenda's father, to stay in Boot on the upper floor of the Post Office, run then by Mary Nolan, the postmistress who, not surprisingly, was well known to everyone in the valley. One evening, once the children were sleeping, we left Brenda's dad in charge and went across the road to the Burnmoor Inn for a drink. There we shared a small room with a conclave of Cumbrian farmers who, from what we could pick up from their broad dialect, were planning the Eskdale show for the following year.

A ghostly Stickle Tarn emerging from the encircling mist
April 1964

For my one day away from the family that week, I drove us all to Wasdale Head where we parted company at noon. I promised to return by 3.00 pm and they would go wherever they wished. Although there was a strong wind in the valley, I was soon sitting just below Napes Needle where I lit a cigarette (tut, tut) without needing to shield the flame of the match. No other climbers were about so I was able to scramble about the lower crags of the Needle unobserved and undisturbed. The two recognised and well-documented rock climbs of Arrowhead and Eagle's Nest ridges beckoned. I would have loved to have climbed Arrowhead but being alone, I thought better of it as I remembered my near fatal slip on Broad Stand. Instead, I scrambled round the base of Tophet Bastion to reach the top of Great Gable by Great Hell Gate and had the summit to myself except for one other devotee of solitude.

By then a wind had begun to blow strongly up the funnel of Ennerdale and I was soon becoming cold. In any case I had no time to linger so ran down the scree to Beckhead, only stopping for a moment to take a photograph of a couple in front of me descending slowly. A minute later, I passed them and reached the family at 2.55 pm. I had climbed my mountain, explored the Napes Ridges and kept my promise not to be late. That evening we shared a splendid farmhouse tea. What more could anyone ask from life?

Kirkfell and Ennerdale from Great Gable
October 1969

YOUTH HOSTELLING

Youth hostels have already featured in these pages starting with my first experience cycling across Yorkshire with my friend, John Shepherd, at the age of fifteen in 1952. During our marriage, as soon as our girls were old enough, Brenda and I began to take them hostelling during their half term holidays from school. Most weekends were enjoyable for no more than being away from the drudgery of everyday life for a short time, but a few youth hostel days stand out either for the weather or for what we achieved.

On Easter Monday 1967, hoping to get away from the Bank Holiday crowds, I drove us all to Settle for a day walking in Attermire and a visit to Victoria Cave located behind and above the town. There are no great hills to boast of thereabouts, but such hills as are there give the appearance of being much grander and higher than they actually are. Consequently, we made what seemed to us to be much faster progress than we expected and enjoyed a magnificent relaxing day far from the nose-to-tail traffic that would be thronging the Lake District. The day was so good that two weeks later we began to make more use of our YHA membership and took the girls for a weekend in Slaidburn for their first time in a hostel. Once again, we encountered the old remembered smell of seasoned timbers, coupled with a hint of stale sweating bodies and well used boots that seem to greet any hosteller arriving at any hostel at the end of any long day.

King's House in Slaidburn was (perhaps is still) the epitome of traditional hostelling, a place devoted to the succour and (at one time alcoholic) refreshment of travellers on the King's Highway. The room to the left of the entrance still had an old oak corner settle on two walls facing the warden's little office and shop. Behind it was a narrow corridor, its walls festooned with posters and adverts for local village hops and social events. A few small ledges displayed a range of stones and fossils from where one curious corner led to the common room where we completed a 1,000 piece jig-saw and played cards and skittles. To the right of the entrance was the warden's kitchen from where there came a never ending flow of music ranging from Beethoven and Mozart to Stravinsky, Schoenberg and Messaien.

The men's dormitory was a barn of a place and morning ablutions were done across the cobbled yard. That first evening was calm and so tranquil that when we walked by the River Hodder, the only sound was the brief splash of our skimming stones. We only had one full day and we used it to explore the area around Stocks reservoir, so for once there were no hills, but an arduous nine mile walk for the children during which we looked for wild-flowers and fossils. By way of stone walls, stiles, fences, copses and hedges we arrived at a small chapel surrounded by massed banks of conifers. We were surprised to find a church so far from any other signs of habitation, but I'd read about Tosside Congregational Chapel and assumed it to be the same. However, subsequent investigation revealed that it was the Dalehead church of St. Mark that had been demolished to make room for Stocks reservoir and rebuilt on its present site in 1932.

After paying brief homage we continued to New House, finding it no longer new but also uninhabited. There was no sign of a bridge when we reached the river which presented us with a problem. I really ought to have checked this before we set out, but I solved it by carrying the others across on my back. At the same time, this also gave some relief to my aching feet.

A year later, in deference to YHA rules, we drove to Eskdale Green to leave the car there and walk the three miles to Eskdale Youth Hostel. The next day we walked over the flank of Harter Fell to Black Hall Farm in the Duddon valley. The adopted hostel at Troutal that I'd used in 1961 had closed. We were surprised to find that three wickets had been set up for a game of impromptu cricket on a bumpy (!!) pitch on the adjoining intake field. But it was good fun. Concurrently, as we played, we heard on the farmer's transistor radio with sadness, that the great Brian Statham was at that moment playing his last match for Lancashire against the old enemy, Yorkshire. At the close of play that day Yorkshire were 34 for 8. Why were we not there at Old Trafford?

We returned to Eskdale the next day by the road over Hardknott. It was a delight to imagine the horrified faces of inexperienced drivers attempting the pass for the first time and we sat for a while watching as some failed to change into bottom gear soon enough and had to reverse ignominiously before taking another run at it. Towards the end of the week the weather was breaking, and we took the girls up Scafell by way of Foxes Tarn and Cam Spout on an overcast but dry day. The next day we all walked to Beckfoot to catch La'al Ratty, I got off at Eskdale |Green to collect the car and the others continued to Ravenglass where I met them before driving home over Corney Fell to Ulpha.

One superb day was devoted to an unexpected ascent of Coniston Old Man in February 1970 when, one morning while staying at Coniston Far End Y.H., we woke to find dazzling sunshine flooding the dormitory as the sun rose over Grizedale Forest. Later, as we walked into the village, we turned a corner and saw a breathtaking view of the Old Man – clothed in fresh snow and looking alpine in its splendour against the brilliant blue of a cloudless sky. It was calling out to be climbed.

Prudence dictated that we take the conventional line of ascent. The sun was blazing down, so walking was hot work as we followed the track upwards to pass through the derelict landscape of Coppermines valley. There was not a breath of wind, and no sound disturbed the silence save the crunch of snow beneath our boots. At about 1600 ft Brenda found a perfect suntrap to rest and Kathryn stayed with her. While there they had an unexpected encounter with a fox while Rosalind and I continued to the summit.

Above Low Water we turned into the shadow of the ridge to find that drifts of snow were lying up to two feet deep in places and the air was very cold with it. In places a hard crust would give way and at others there was only powder snow too cold to coalesce to an icy firmness. The view eastwards was beautiful beyond belief with the Howgills standing crystal clear in the stillness. Rosalind needed a hand in places as the ascent grew steeper, and in others progress was impossible owing to a glassy hardness that didn't bode well for anyone foolish enough to try standing on it. We made use of any exposed dry rock that we came across and kicked steps where it wasn't, eventually reaching the summit safely. The sky was a deeper blue than I had ever seen and the snow clad Scafells away to the west looked superb in their comparative isolation. An immense cornice hung from the lip of Brim Fell and a wind began to sweep up from Low Water gathering strength like an express train. We descended rapidly, speedily, haphazardly. We jumped, we ran, we slithered, we shouted and we laughed – ours were the first footsteps to be left in that pristine white world. Later there would be others but we had been the first! Life at that moment could not have been better. Two hours later, from the Coniston road, I looked back to see black dots high in that other world. For a moment I envied them their position before recalling that Rosalind and I had trodden there on snow not then defiled by human feet – we had had the best of it.

Coniston Old Man
February 1970

89

During her school days, Brenda had joined the 4th Wigan Town (High School) Girl Guide Company and had been presented with her Queen's Guide Award. In 1967 she had assisted Barbara, the wife of the recently appointed minister of our church to set up a Brownie Pack which was soon followed by a Guide Company. By September 1970 the YHA regulations were less stringent than ten years earlier so when somebody suggested that we should take some of the guides to the Lake District to stay for two nights at Ambleside Y.H. I was more than happy to assist with leading a walk. I had hopes of repeating the ascent of Jack's Rake so we took the bus up the Langdale valley to the New Dungeon Ghyll hotel and we all climbed by Mill Gill to Stickle Tarn where we stopped for lunch and I explained the options.

Not surprisingly there was a range of abilities, not to mention interests, so we split up and agreed to meet later. Brenda led some back down by Mill Gill, my experienced friend (another John) took one party round the right flank of Pavey Ark and I led three of the guides – Rosalind, Sheena and Margaret, up Jack's Rake to meet the others at the top. I doubt if the Guide Association would have approved but this was a church outing and not a Guiding event. The second day we walked over Loughrigg and called in at the big cave, easily visible then from the road on the far side of Rydal Water until a stand of conifers grew large enough to obscure it. We made our way back to Ambleside by way of Pelter Bridge and the road past Fox How, built by Thomas Arnold, famous as the headmaster of Rugby School, on whom Thomas Hughes based his story *Tom Brown's School Days*. His son, the famous poet Matthew Arnold also used the house as a holiday retreat.

By 1971, both girls had added Elterwater in Langdale, Grinton Lodge in Swaledale and Ingleton to their list of hostels and Kathryn had also stayed at Barrow House in Borrowdale (while Rosalind was away on holiday with school). In October, Brenda and Barbara, Tawny Owl and Brown Owl respectively for the 9th Wigan West (Bispham Methodist) Brownies, attended the Association of Methodist Scouters and Guiders (AMSAG) annual conference at Gilwell.

I arranged to take Rosalind and Kathryn for two nights at Honister Y.H. It would prove to be a very wet weekend. On the way there, we stopped at the top of Newlands Hause to admire the spectacular waterfalls of Moss Force from both sides by climbing up one bank, crossing the stream at the top and descending by the other bank. We arrived at the hostel in a rather wet and sorry condition. That night we were wakened several times by wind and rain battering the hostel and we were not impressed by the torrential rain that was still falling at first light.

However, after breakfast, it began to slacken off so we (that is I) decided that we would climb Great Gable. After all, at the top of Honister we were already almost half-way up. We were adequately clothed, though perhaps we could have worn more suitable waterproofs bought expensively from a specialist supplier. Rain fell on and off all the way as we approached Green Gable following the line of Moses' Trod. Below Green Gable, we met one tremendous hurricane that all but destroyed such plastic mac coverings as we had. We could only stand with our backs to the storm and wait for it to abate. We ate lunch at (of all places) Windy Gap which was surprisingly almost wind free. From there, we remained in cloud as we crossed over the summit and began our descent to Styhead Tarn, now in relative calm, probably shielded by the bulk of the mountain.

Moreover, the rain now seemed to have stayed in the clouds. Styhead though was a different matter. The tops of the waves on Styhead Tarn were blown off as they raced across the surface, and we could feel the spray 100 yards away. At least it was now behind us as we descended to Seathwaite. We then had a long doleful trudge up the road back to the hostel and, knowing that we would be early and that hostel rules dictated that we could only enter after it opened at 5.00 pm, I wondered what we would find to do. But we'd been seen by the friendly warden and as he helped us to remove our wet boots and soaking socks, he referred to us as heroes. He even helped us to wring out our wet clothes before we made use of the drying room.

I was sleeping well that night until the warden woke me at 2.00 am to say that a police constable had driven up to deliver a message that Brenda had had an asthma attack at Gilwell and was now in the Royal Albert Edward Infirmary (RAEI) in Wigan. Fortunately, there was then an AA box (and phone of course) on the roadside by the hostel and, being a member, I had a key and was able to arrange a rendezvous for the next day with the RAEI in place of another day in the Lake District for which I'd been hoping.

New Year, 1972 saw us at Longthwaite Y.H. in Borrowdale for a weekend and who should we find there but our friendly warden from Honister, helping out while Honister was closed for the winter. The weather was too bad for the higher fells, so we contented ourselves with the adjacent Castle Crag. For the February half term break we had much better weather and stayed at the recently-built Patterdale hostel. We stopped at the top of Kirkstone Pass, where copious amounts of snow had fallen, to watch several skiers who were clearly making the most of it. There were dark clouds over Helvellyn on the Sunday, so we walked over Boardale Hause to Sandwick and returned along the Ullswater shore watching the evening shadows lengthen as the lights of Glenridding winked at us across the lake.

Shafts of brilliant early morning sunshine the next day augured well for the rest of the day, so we left the car at Glenridding lead mines with Helvellyn in our sights. Because of the depth of new snow, I thought it better to use what I call "the easy way" up the zig-zags on the gentle slopes of Raise. Well over half-way up the zig-zags we stopped to dig a snow hole for shelter because Kathryn had started to feel cold. We ate our lunch there before Brenda and Kathryn decided to return to the car while I carried on with Rosalind, having arranged to meet the others on Keldas.

We might have been in the Alps as range after range of snow-covered mountains stretched away to the Pennines in the distance far beyond the dark trench that contained Ullswater. As we approached the main ridge, I noticed that what had been soft deep snow lower down was changing to ice on the south facing slope, probably due to previously melted snow having frozen overnight. Although we were not in a potentially fatal situation, a slip could still have serious consequences on a convex slope that descended 1,000 ft below us. The frozen crust was a delight to kick steps into and for the first time I used Rosalind's long scarf in place of a rope to tie us together wrist to wrist. We made for the flatter more level ground above and were soon looking over Western Lakeland.

On the top of Whiteside we experienced a whiteout with no reference to anything about us except each other as we climbed what could have been a giant iced wedding cake. Eventually we emerged into brilliant sunshine with Catstye Cam etched sharply against the deep blue of the afternoon sky. We were soon in cloud again but a few exposed rocks on the plateau helped with the next whiteout and we never saw Striding Edge – but I had no intention of attempting that route anyway under such conditions. That was a place for true mountaineers with their ice axes and crampons. I kept us well away from the eastern crags fearing the possibility of a cornice and we came down to Patterdale by way of Grizedale Tarn and met Brenda and Kathryn on Keldas within 5 minutes of my estimated time.

Keldas, one of the loveliest places in the Lake District
April 6th 2004

Later that year, in August, we returned to Honister Y.H, where we left the car at the start of what we intended to be a short week. The weather was no better than in 1971, but we left the hostel after the first night to climb directly up Dalehead and reached Hindscarth in driving rain before deciding to descend to Buttermere Y.H. The next day was equally bad, so I left the others in Buttermere village and started to walk back up the pass to bring the car down. I'd mentioned to my mum and dad what we were doing before we'd left home and as they'd driven up to the Lakes for a day out, by coincidence or good fortune, they were driving down the pass to look for us and saw me trudging up. Naturally, we all got together then, hoping to find a rain free spot near Loweswater. Rain continued to follow us the next day and, being booked in at Wasdale Y.H. I took Rosalind over Scarth Gap and Black Sail passes to Wasdale Head while Brenda drove Kathryn round to meet us. From the hostel we had a low level walk over Irton Pike and back, but the final day would prove to be the best of the week.

The girls wanted a day pony trekking in Eskdale so I got them to drop me off at Bowderdale at the foot of Yewbarrow. Much against Mr. Wainwright's advice, instead of following the well-worn path up Yewbarrow that goes to the left of Bell Rib, I went "off piste" to the right. I wanted more than an easy walk with no excitement; I needed something more akin to Jack's Rake on Pavey Ark. I then spent a happy half hour or so scrambling up Bell Rib by whatever seemed to be the most interesting route that I'd arrived at. As far as I was concerned, nobody might have ever trod where I was treading. There were no problems and no tricky situations that couldn't be resolved by back tracking if I felt the need. The sun was shining, and the rocks were dry.

It was a wonderful day and I was soon over Yewbarrow and ascending Red Pike making for the "chair". This is a man-made stone structure large enough to accommodate a giant, and in Victorian times, tourists would say they were going to climb "The Chair", the nickname by which Red Pike was then known. From there I continued to Scoat Fell, including a short detour to the top of Steeple and so on to Haycock and the final summit of the day – Seatallan. Between Scoat Fell and Haycock I met the only people I saw that day, four walkers on their way from Gillerthwaite Y.H. at the foot of Ennerdale to Wasdale Y.H..

By the time I began the last climb up Seatallan, I was beginning to tire but at the top I was rewarded by the most extensive view that I have ever seen. After the rain of the previous three days, the air was so clear that there was no doubt I could see England, Ireland, Scotland and Wales. The Isle of Man looked poised high enough to slide down the slope of the Irish Sea as if to crash against the Cumbrian coast, while far beyond it a thin line of hills closed off the western sky. Not being sure of my geography, I took a compass bearing wondering if it might be the Mull of Galloway (how wrong I was). When I checked later, I realised that beyond the Isle of Man I'd seen the Mourne Mountains of Northern Ireland, the highest being Slieve Donard about 108 miles away. The air was so still that I heard the sound of La'al Ratty's whistle as clearly as if I'd been waiting on the platform for it to arrive at Eskdale Green station.

Seatallan has an unnatural (and unusual) feature in that the summit is crowned with an inexplicably inordinate number of stones piled high into a huge cairn. Mr. Wainwright notes that it is variously described as an ancient cairn or tumulus and that local archaeologists describe it as a large tumulus. Whatever the case, it must have had some significance for the early settlers in the area and may be thousands of years old.

The way off the fell was obvious and I was soon reunited with my family on the road close to the farm at Windsor after another magnificent exploration of the lesser-known Western Fells.

The dramatic view of the head of Wastwater from Great Door
The rocks of Bell Rib on the right
August 7th 1975

Seatallan

Descending the fell at the loose end
of an Autumn day, hanging
on the slack warm air
over the sun washed hills
came the warning call
of the miniature train.

La'al Ratty's rattling racks had arrived,
invisible at Eskdale Green. Far away,
above and beyond a distant isle, precarious
on the slope of the western sea
Slieve Donard smudged the horizon's rim.

No breath of wind disturbed the peace.
No sound but skylarks lost in space
as darkness, slowly climbing
wrapped the summit tumulus in night,

sole witness to the forgotten weight
of alien feet that once paced out
this place, perhaps on guard. Not even grass
would dare to whisper then.

By 1975, we had used hostels at Ambleside (again), Llangollen, Longthwaite (again), Windermere (previously known as Troutbeck), Crowcombe in the Quantocks, St Briavels in Gloucestershire, Ludlow and Esthwaite Lodge (again) but had climbed nothing of note. Our girls were no longer content always to be led by their parents and were naturally becoming more independent, but we had one last trip to stay at Coniston Far End Y.H. where, for the first time we had a four-bed dormitory to ourselves. Perhaps that was our first introduction to the development of youth hostels into something more akin to a small guest house. From there I took Rosalind over Wetherlam while

Brenda took Kathryn to explore the hidden beauty of Tilberthwaite. On another day I took Rosalind up the Old Man from Boo Tarn in driving snow that was as bad as anything I'd ever known. Later that year the girls went hostelling on their own in the Lake District during an August heat wave while Brenda and I enjoyed the luxury of a week at the Woolpack Inn in Eskdale. The times – they were a-changing!

We never again hostelled as a family, but Brenda and I remained members of the YHA for many years and would use hostels as a convenience, especially in Scotland where accommodation in remote locations was then very limited. The hostels at Ullapool and Torridon were our favourites.

YHA membership was particularly useful when, having begun to enter fell races, in 1990, I entered the Chevy Chase race that began at Wooler YH and was organised then, and for many subsequent years, by Lawrence Heslop who became, and still is, a good friend. We would stay for two nights, usually with a bedroom to ourselves, and eventually began to assist in a minor way by helping to clean up after the two to three hundred runners and walkers had left.

FELL RUNNING

I have often wondered what is meant by the "mid-life crisis". As far as I can tell, it hasn't happened to me yet, although I grant that at about the age of forty, I began to think that I had better take more care of my body. It wasn't exactly a sudden decision – I'd stopped smoking a few years earlier thinking that Rosalind and Kathryn were approaching the age when they might take up the filthy habit and I could hardly admonish them if I were smoking myself. I only drank alcohol in moderation and my diet was, I thought, well balanced and nourishing. I can't really explain why I began to exercise more than I had previously. I didn't join a gym. I don't think they were around at that time, at any rate not many. In any case it would have cost money that I didn't want to pay when I could buy a pair of running shoes that would last for as long (almost) as I wished. I soon discovered that running shoes don't last forever – I've since gone through several pairs as improved materials and designs have come on to the market.

But one day, for no other reason than curiosity, as an experiment I put on my tennis shoes and decided to see how long it would take me to run three to four miles. That would be enough to start. I measured the road distance with a tiny, wheeled map measurer that I'd bought many years before for using on my Lake District maps. My first outing was a great disappointment. A quarter of a mile from home, despite feeling good for the first two hundred yards, I was out of breath and gasping like a stranded fish. I soon learned not to set off too fast. On that occasion I could only manage to jog on a flat road surface at a little over my usual walking pace. On anything with a slight incline, I was reduced to a breathless plod. My calculations back home showed that it had taken me between twelve and fifteen minutes to cover a mile. Hardly a challenge to Roger Bannister. However, I persisted, though on a somewhat erratic basis and after several weeks my times for a set distance reduced to what I thought was an acceptable level. I bought Jim Fixx's book on running and realised there was more to running than merely putting one foot in front of the other and I began to set myself some target times.

It seemed rather strange that running seemed then to be taking off by others besides me, and a magazine appeared in, I think, the 1970s devoted entirely to running. I read every issue from cover to cover, bought proper running shoes for training and a special pair of lightweight shoes for road races. These were my favourite shoes known as ASICS Tigers. Each shoe weighed less than 200 grams and they were so comfortable that putting them on felt like donning a pair of gloves, so perfect was the fit. They were relatively expensive, so I rarely wore them for training runs. I began to increase my distances and, depending on how I felt, would go out to run where the fancy took me. Local roads, cart tracks, hills or country lanes all provided me with a variety of distances and terrains, though I seldom had enough opportunities to run more than three or four times a week.

I soon learned about the finer points of training – aerobic and anaerobic, interval training, how to lose weight, how to increase leg muscle strength and the need for carbohydrate loading to avoid "hitting the wall" on long distances. I also began to do short runs during my lunchtime breaks, but while my speed improved, I could never maintain anything better than a seven-minute mile pace over a long distance. The first London marathon was held in 1981, by which time I was aged 44 and by my reckoning I wasn't up to running that distance. On the other hand, when I watched the race on telly, I realised I wouldn't have been by any means the last to finish. So later that year I entered the first "Pony" marathon that began and ended in Bolton. I finished about halfway down the list of finishers which I thought wasn't too bad at my age. I also knew then that I would never have a chance of winning such road races.

But the fells were a different matter. The Fell Running Association (FRA) had been formed on April 4th, 1970, at Whitehough Camp School, previously the Barley Y.H. where Brenda and I had stayed in 1956. The FRA was soon organising races throughout the country, many being in the Lake District. This would become a means to an end, so I joined the FRA and also the nearest fell running club – Horwich RMI which had begun as an athletic club for the Horwich Railway Men's Institute. Most fell runners join a club, but anyone could enter a fell race regardless. In my case it was an excuse to get on to the fells and cover distances far greater than I had ever dreamed of, without leaving Brenda alone for too long wandering round the shops of Ambleside or Keswick.

FRA membership also gave me annual access to the fell running calendar. Apart from the aesthetic attraction that mountains have for me, fell running, like orienteering, needs navigational skills on wet or misty days. There are nowadays several fell races held during most weeks of the year, but because of other commitments, over the next ten years I only entered about ten races per year. Mostly these were no more than an excuse to spend a day or part thereof amongst hills and mountains with no expectation of winning, which I guess was the same for ninety percent of the other entrants. Anyway, in my case I considered myself to be fell running – not fell racing. It was a chance to meet and occasionally chat to my heroes – at that time runners such as Joss Naylor, Billy Bland, Kenny Stuart and Ron Hill. On one race – The Three Shires, for a short distance I found myself running alongside Chris Brasher, famous for pacing Roger Bannister's four-minute mile and a co-founder of the London marathon with the Olympian John Disley.

My first experience of a fell race was at Kentmere in April 1982. There were over 300 starters and anyone watching the start would have known that I had little idea of what to expect for I was wearing some of my old clothes including a tattered woollen pullover and wind proof top for warmth and I carried a bottle of water against possible dehydration. The more experienced runners wore shorts and T-shirts and carried all they needed in bum-bags. It was a clear day on the tops so there were no navigational problems and although I was one of the last to finish, I was happy enough. By my standards I had had a good day out over Kentmere Pike, High Street and Ill Bell, eleven miles in a little over two hours.

The same race the following year, held again in April was an entirely different affair. The tops were all in cloud and even at the start, by St. Cuthbert's Church in Kentmere, rain was falling. This time, with a year of experience behind me, I looked at the dark clouds above and decided to wear top and bottom thermal underwear, tracksters (elasticated lightweight trousers) and full body hooded waterproofs. That may seem to be a case of over kill, and as I looked at some of the other three hundred and seventy competitors in vests and shorts, I began to wonder if I was right. I was soon running amongst the tail enders and had to queue at the first congested stile on the way up Kentmere Pike. By the time we were nearing the summit, what had been rain in the valley had changed to wet snow and a few of the lightly clad runners in vests and shorts appeared out of the mist on their way back to the start, muttering foul imprecations about the weather. Soon there seemed to be a mass evacuation of the mountain but a few of us continued and, for myself, I had no intention of giving in. Shades of my Outward Bound training?

Conditions on the fell tops were truly horrendous. A gale force wind was driving snow parallel to the hillside up out of Kentmere and plastered my left side with a layer of ice while leaving my other side totally dry. I was now alone and at one point, to escape the constant onslaught of wind driven snow, I had to stop running and crouch down in a shallow depression to let the storm rage over my head. But I was intent on finishing, so I carried on, navigating by compass through what had become a total whiteout and reached the Nan Bield Pass exactly where I wanted to be, but still alone. Finding High Street from there was no problem and I was soon on Ill Bell where the storm was raging so furiously that I had to climb the final hundred feet on all fours holding on to whatever rock or tussock of frozen grass I could find. Back at the finish I learned that 188 runners, more than half the field, had retired. It was difficult not to feel smug!

Fell races fall into three categories based on their length – long medium and short. Each category is further divided into three – A,

B or C depending on the amount of ascent involved, "A" being the category involving most. Thus, the hardest, longest races are classified as "A long". The sport as we know it today is usually considered to have begun in connection with country fairs at which various competitions involving physical strength were held. In the Lake District, the Grasmere Fair today involves hound trails and Cumberland wrestling as well as a fell race.

In the early days, the races were known as "Guides' Races", the one for Grasmere involving the ascent and descent of Butter Crag on the ridge leading to Fairfield. The runners were largely visible throughout the course of the race that would usually be over in under twenty minutes. The record for that race was set by Fred Reeves at 12 minutes 21.6 seconds in 1978, but in 1985, Kenny Stuart set a new record of 12 minutes and 1 second for the race, its name having been changed to the Grasmere Amateur Course. Human nature being what it is, short fell races became a popular spectator sport on which considerable amounts of money might change hands. In addition, the winners of the many Guides' Races received prize money and so were classed as professionals. At the Clynnog village fair in North Wales, in 1969, I became a professional runner by winning sixpence (two and a half pence) for coming third in a 200-metre sprint across a field where thistles had grown to a most uncomfortable and embarrassing height. I have never divulged this to the FRA, though I doubt if it would have affected my amateur status.

As mentioned above, the FRA that began in 1970 was an amateur organisation with simple rules that placed the onus of responsibility for their own safety on each competitor. In other words, "You enter at your own risk." However, with the passage of time, due partly to a very few regrettable deaths, usually due to inexperience, the rules have become more stringent. Today the FRA Handbook includes not only fourteen pages of rules (including three pages of rule changes for 2021), but also articles on Parental Consent (for junior races), the FRA Welfare Policy, the FRA Photography and Social Media Policy, Land Access and Environmental Considerations, as well as Insurance and Hypothermia.

Short races never appealed to me – they were over too quickly. I much preferred the "A" or "B" longer ones when I could be out on the fells for up to five hours. "Running" is perhaps not the best word to use in my case for I could only walk up a fell side, jog on the tops and run when descending. I know that is also the case for many others because I've often been part of a multi-coloured crocodile of runners ascending a steep slope. Only elite runners, expecting to finish in a little over an hour would run up such slopes as Mouldry Bank at the start of the Coniston race. My time for that race was usually about an hour and three quarters, but I was always, (with a few exceptions referred to later) about half-way down (or up) the finishers list.

The only constant for any race is the route (unless access is refused by a landowner) but the race itself is naturally subject to the vagaries of the weather. I entered the Coniston race thirteen times over the years and on different occasions experienced blistering sunshine, snow-storms and thick mist. I usually enjoyed any race when thick cloud enveloped the tops, but one time on Coniston when visibility was down to about ten yards, I forgot my rule to trust myself and, instead of following the ridge to the top of the Old Man, I followed a group descending towards Levers Water. About twenty runners were already a long way below me before I realised their (and my) error, so I shouted down to them before climbing hurriedly back to the ridge while cursing myself for my stupidity.

The "A" long Borrowdale race (17 miles/6,500 ft) was one of my favourites because it takes in the major peaks of the central Lake District including Scafell Pike and Great Gable. In 1983, the weather was so hot that over 50 runners retired, probably from dehydration. But in the same race in 1986, I needed to crouch on hands and knees to escape from the wind as I crossed Styhead. Later during that race, I slipped while running on easy ground on Brandreth with the wind behind me, sat on my left ankle and fractured the lower tip of my left tibia. I managed to hobble to the Honister Pass check point where I met Brenda who'd heard the news relayed to the finish by the Honister Pass marshals. Three weeks later, I was able to resume running and training again. Meanwhile I'd managed to continue aerobic training by cycling every day using only my right leg.

Winter Hill, being close at hand, was another favourite. I could run over the moors whenever I had some spare time and learn the topography until it was imprinted on my memory. Because I'd joined Horwich RMI, I wore my Horwich vest for races. Visitors from afar would recognise my vest and follow me, thinking that I knew the best routes. This invariably happened on foggy days when one patch of moorland was indistinguishable from every other. For me, this was both annoying and satisfying. On the one hand, they would invariably leave me behind as we neared the finish but on the other, it meant that I had demonstrated the value of "local knowledge". One incident really pleased me when, with a coterie of runners behind me, we met another group heading in completely the wrong direction. Some of my followers decided they'd had enough of me and deserted to follow the other group. That was a good moment.

Three Shires fell race runners assembling at the start
September 1992

I always enjoyed The Three Shires race that starts from the Inn of the same name in Little Langdale. The day of the race in 1991 was reasonably dry but was overcast. There was low cloud on Wetherlam and the higher rocks were wet and slippery. I was having a good race until, approaching the summit cairn on Pike O' Blisco, I slipped and fell heavily on to my back. When I stood up, I thought I had blood running down my legs, but quickly realised that I'd squashed the Ribena packet that was in my bum bag. With some relief, I carried on easily then by running down to Blea Tarn, but once I began the final climb up Lingmoor, I began to have chest pains that would take three weeks to disappear. I've since thought the pain could have been caused by a fractured rib on my right side.

There's nothing wrong with retiring from a fell race. Even Outward Bound alumni know what prudence is on mountains – a desire to continue living. I once retired from a Winter Hill race because I was so cold. I knew that if I continued, I would become hypothermic. My knees had already turned blue, and I was shivering uncontrollably. On the other hand, when I entered the Ennerdale race in 1986, (the longest and hardest in the FRA calendar at 23 miles with 7,500 ft of ascent), I retired in consideration of the marshals. Two hours into the race I knew if I continued, I would be "timed out" and so expected to retire. It was a lovely day and at least I'd had a good day walking and jogging over the Buttermere Fells as far as the Blackbeck Tarn check-point. There I rested for a while and chatted to the marshals before I had a lovely, unhurried walk down to the finish at the Ennerdale Lake outlet, passing by Black Sail Hut and through the forest. On my way, I was passed by a Land Rover carrying other runners who'd continued and had been timed out, probably at Green Gable summit. They offered me a lift, but I preferred the solitude and the silence of the forest.

Although the fell running fraternity now has over seven thousand members, the true heroes of the movement are the marshals who establish themselves at check points well before any runners pass through and remain there in all weathers until everyone is accounted for. It is to them I give my thanks for all the happy days I've spent amongst the hills (mostly in the Lake District), pushing myself towards my limit as far as I comfortably could.

Relaxing after the Coniston race
May 3rd 1997

HELVELLYN BY NIGHT

Glenridding lay sleeping. In the depths of the blackness an unseen dog bayed at the full moon, the sound seeming to hang on the still air. Earlier that evening I had risen silently, dressed myself and, quietly closing the cottage door, had crossed the gravel in stockinged feet before donning my boots by the yard gate. This was to be, as far as I could see, my last chance for that year to fulfil what had become an annual pilgrimage to the summit of Helvellyn. We had rented the cottage (pre-Wainwright) for the October half-term – £9.00 a week and collect your own firewood. For once, bad weather had kept the high fells out of bounds, especially for the children, but on the Friday with the last-minute shopping done and the bags packed, the rain stopped and by evening the wind had eased and the sky was clearing.

I looked longingly at the fells and when Brenda suggested that there was still time if I went by night, my mind was made up. After all, I knew the mountain well, if not intimately. The weather forecast was fine for the next day or so; I had a powerful torch and there would be a full moon. Secretly I thought that the authorities and the Mountain Rescue services would disapprove but I would take all the normal precautions – map, compass, whistle etc. and I had often walked alone. I considered the additional risk introduced by the absence of daylight to be minimal.

There was no path beyond the yard gate and I climbed directly up the face of Birkhouse Moor. I had left the cottage at the witching hour; the moon was full and clear and there was no need for the torch. I knew there were a few scattered crags above, but I had seen them over the past week and they could easily be circumvented. At first, I was disturbed when mysterious grey shapes that materialised out of the shadows began to stir but they were only recumbent sheep and they shuffled reluctantly out of my path. I was going well when I heard the dog bark, the distant sound emphasizing the solitude, and from that moment the silence became almost tangible – no birds sang, no streams tinkled, no gentle zephyrs rustled the dying autumn bracken. Even my own footsteps went unheard on the wet grass.

In the distance, the silvered whaleback bulk of Striding Edge appeared like an old friend, darkness dropping away on either hand into impenetrable depths which the pencilled beam of my torch was powerless to penetrate. On such a silvery pavement, poised above Stygian blackness, no man (or woman) ever walked. Time sped effortlessly on, so by what means I reached the far end of Striding Edge I will never know. By then I was in a state of semi-enchantment. I knew only that there, for the first time, I would need to use the torch. So, carefully examining the short scramble that in daylight is so easy, I tied the torch to my waist band and climbed down, one step at a time, taking stock of my position at each step. My fears had been unjustified for a few minutes later I took refuge in a fissure on Helvellyn's flank against a cold breeze that had sprung up out of Nethermost Cove. From there, the character of the night changed entirely. The wind pursued me to the summit where the cold struck through my anorak as the icy fingers of a swirling mist closed round me, and the moon, although now invisible, shed a silvery radiance over every stone and blade of grass, clothing the very air with a silken lustre.

I rested in the lee of the summit shelter, thinking of the dog that had barked in the night and the spirit of the hills and wondering what had compelled me to climb Helvellyn alone at night under a full moon. Such questions are probably better left unasked for I reached no conclusion. Those moments, however, were timeless in their quality and for how long I sat there, I cannot recall for time had ceased to exist. I was not conscious of sound for there was no sound; I experienced no movement for nothing moved; no wind fanned my cheek, and I knew that I had tasted of that mystical quality that only mountains can give. Not there was the magical parting of mist curtains that once revealed to me the length of Borrowdale from Great End, nor even the joyful sunburst after rain on Red Pike. Here was peace and solitude, deep and lasting, timeless and eternal in its message.

Soon I was walking west-northwest by compass taking care to avoid the crags which I knew to be on my right while debating with myself the relative wisdom of descending by Swirral Edge and Catstye Cam by moonlight or taking the safer way by Keppel Cove. Valour submitted to prudence, and I crossed the summit of Helvellyn's Lower Man to follow the ridge northward as far as the col between Lower Man and Whiteside. There I turned eastward to descend the steep grassy slopes of Brown Cove. Once more in moonlight with the grassy tussocks as regular as a staircase I soon reached the tennis court smoothness of the remains of Keppel Cove tarn while recalling the joy of ascending Catstye Cam's snow-covered northwest ridge the previous year. At the same time, I had been looking for signs of the breached dam with the intention of using it to cross the stream and thought I saw it 300 feet or so below me. Impossible I thought but continued down. Within some twenty or thirty paces I all but walked into the back face of the dam which now towered above me and I realised that I had in fact seen the breach at the bottom of the dam wall. My laughter disturbed the silence, and I retraced my steps, avoiding as best I could the boggy ground into which I had strayed. I used the torch again while crossing the dam, for having safely negotiated Striding Edge by moonlight it would have been ridiculous to become a mountain rescue statistic by falling from a man-made structure. The course of Glenridding beck was easy to follow and it seemed that in no time I had reached the lead mines and the youth hostel.

Four hours after leaving the cottage I was unlacing my boots by the yard gate, enriched by a store of new memories to sustain me through the long winter nights. Brenda heard my return as I entered, and we shared a cup of tea before a few hours of sleep and the long drive South.

THE YORKSHIRE THREE PEAKS

The circuit of Ingleborough, Whernside and Pen-y-Ghent is a walk well known to lovers of hills and mountains. It is not specifically a challenge although many who set out know before they lace up their boots or trainers, that it will tax their abilities, in many cases to the utmost. The distance is today usually reckoned to be twenty-three miles and the total height climbed about 4,500 ft. It's possible to begin at several points along the route but most people choose to start at Horton in Ribblesdale (referred to from here as "Horton") where there is plenty of parking space. Walkers can clock in with a card at the local café and have it stamped as a record of their day out when they return.

It was not always thus. A Dalesman Publishing Company pamphlet of 1949 reports that in July 1887, two masters from Giggleswick School, Canon J.R. Wynne-Edwards and D.R. Smith completed the first round to include the three summits by starting and ending their walk at the school. They estimated the distance to have been 27 miles. A later Dalesman pamphlet *The Three Peaks – A Dalesman Picture Guide*, published in 1962 states that they took 14 hours which by today's times would suggest that they were out for a pleasant stroll, albeit a long one. Other starting points such as Ingleton and Clapham have also been reported together with a variety of times.

By 1949, members of the Yorkshire Climbers' Club were becoming competitive and times for the circuit began to fall to the extent that the Dalesman pamphlet of that year recorded in bold type that **"Desmond Birch made a complete circuit in 4 hours 27 minutes."** By 1954, the Three Peaks race, starting at the Hill Inn at the foot of Ingleborough, had been established. There were only eight starters in that inaugural race! But the sport of fell running had taken off and eight years later sixty-eight runners were on the starting line and the record time stood at 2 hrs 58 mins and 45 seconds. Today, the popularity of fell running is such that the entry list is frequently oversubscribed. The record time of 2 hrs 29 mins and 53 seconds for that route was set by Geoff Norman in

1974 and is unlikely ever to be beaten owing to difficulties over access to private land that have caused the route to be lengthened. At the time of writing, the current record time over the present route, set in 1996 by Andy Peace, is 2 hrs 46 mins 3 seconds.

I have never attempted the race, knowing that I would probably be too slow and therefore "timed out" before I reached the finish inside the required time of 4 hours 30 minutes. My fastest circuit (at the age of 47) was 4 hours 48 minutes in June 1984. If only I'd taken up fell running when I was much younger! But for many years the circuit became a favourite annual outing for me with a variety of friends. Between 1979 and 2000 I completed the round 19 times. One year I missed the outing because I was working in India, and the year after that, I had to retire because I'd returned from India totally out of condition. For one thing, there were no Indian hills high enough where I was working on which I could keep fit. Also, the weather in India was far too hot for serious running, even at 6.00 am.

On the circuit mentioned above when I retired, I was accompanied by Kathryn, who by then was a fell runner in her own right. We set off from Ribblehead travelling anti-clockwise, that being my preference because it gets Whernside, generally reckoned to be the least popular peak, out of the way first. By the time we'd crossed over Ingleborough to Horton where Brenda was waiting with the car, I was totally exhausted and gave in. A year later I had recovered enough to walk round in 7 hours, but I was by then fifteen years older than I was for my first (failed) attempt in 1977 which is worth relating so here it is.

In the August of 1977, I drove to Horton expecting a rendezvous with two of my work colleagues Patrick (Pat) and John at 8.30 am. By 9.40 nobody had turned up and I was already two hundred yards along the road, having decided to start alone, when I saw them drive past me and on to the car park. It was not an auspicious start to the day. A little over an hour later we had climbed Pen-y-Ghent, expecting to find a long boggy walk to Whernside before us, but John was finding it hard, and someone had told him about the miseries of Black Dub Moss ahead of us.

112

He decided to drop out when we reached the main road and return to Horton. It's not usually advisable to separate a party in that way but we'd had a discussion and decided that John would drive to meet us at Chape-le-Dale while Pat and I continued over Whernside. If we then wished to continue over Ingleborough, he would drive back to Horton. This was to prove a wise move.

Pat and I battled on in driving rain through thigh deep bogs to Ribblehead beyond which we had to search back and forth along a fence line to find the start of the ascent of Whernside. Eventually we found a stile and ascended by a direct line that ended almost exactly on the summit. By the time we had dropped down to Chapel-le-Dale we too had had enough of the rain, the gale force winds and the bogs. Fortunately, as we expected, John was waiting in his car to drive me back to my own car – still at Horton. So ended my first attempt at the Yorkshire Three Peaks but I had learned something about the route, the terrain and the quagmires to be avoided.

The next year was in some ways no different, although in November 1978 I very nearly completed the full circuit. We had missed out Ingleborough the year before, so I decided we'd start from Chapel-le-Dale and climb that mountain first. Also, I conceded a 9.00 am start for the lads, but again I had to wait until 09.45 before they appeared so it was another late start, rendering Whernside an impossibility in the time, even if the weather allowed. However, it was a day of showers interspersed with periods of bright sunshine. We climbed into cloud as soon as we began, and I needed the compass to get us off Ingleborough safely and down to Horton by sundry paths, but we wasted much time in the process. By the time we reached Horton we were two and a half hours behind my schedule and the other two decided to call it a day and let me go on alone.

I left Horton at 2.30 pm and climbed Pen-y-Ghent easily enough without incident, but torrential rain began as I half remembered the route to Ribblehead. I encountered some absolutely murderous bogs that might have claimed me but, thankfully, didn't. At one point I'd taken a couple of steps forward into a bog before I realised it was deeper than I'd expected. As I tried to extricate myself, I looked up and to my horror saw that close by me were the remains of a dead sheep that had been unable to escape the clutches of the mid-thigh deep mud. I was, of course, alone, so that was a timely warning of the dangers of becoming hopelessly bog-bound.

The rain continued most of the way to Ribblehead where I stopped for a drink of hot sweet tea at the mobile shop. That tea was a lifesaver and with Whernside out of contention I enjoyed a gentle stroll back to the car along the road in a state of stupefied euphoria as the Western sky cleared to reveal the Lakeland fells etched against an amber sky. For some inexplicable reason the lads had left a half empty (or should it be half full) bottle of Cointreau against the car; I shouldn't really have tasted it before driving home having been walking for almost nine hours, but I couldn't resist.

I had now climbed every one of the three so I could remember most of the route and there should be no problem for my third attempt a year later. Owing to various commitments and holidays, it was November 21st before I had an opportunity, but I was now accompanied by another friend, Stuart, who was a serious marathon runner with times well below 3 hours. I had also learned much about my fitness – surely this time we would succeed.

Because of the short November days, I'd arranged a 7.30 am start from Horton with Stuart, but once again I was about to set off alone when he turned up at 8.00 am. The weather wasn't too bad with only a few showers that didn't last long. Underfoot though, the boggy stretches were really bad. Despite that, we made good time over Pen-y-Ghent and Whernside until at the start of the last steep climb up Ingleborough, Stuart asked for a rest and lay down on top of a dry stone wall. That was the only reasonably dry place to be found but must have been very uncomfortable. Anyway, he was soon ready to be off again, and we finished the ascent as the evening light began to fade.

We still had about five miles of descent ahead of us and I soon

114

had my torch out. I had previously used Mr Wainwright's guide as he describes the route in his *Walks in Limestone Country* and so took Stuart towards Beecroft Hall (which nobody does now). We walked the last two miles in almost total darkness. My torch had sprung apart above Horton quarry, and we couldn't find the parts. At that time, we didn't know we could have used the now familiar and easier path across the intake fields. We reached Horton at 7.30 pm after 9 hours walking with only two short stops and I was happy. I'd completed the full circuit, albeit at the third attempt.

By July 1982, I'd completed two marathons so a family trip to the Three Peaks gave me a chance to find out how I would fare on a route that I now knew quite well. I no longer looked on it as a walk. This was to be a run/walk depending on how I felt within the bounds of comfort. The rest of the family all did their own thing.

I started at the Hill Inn at Chapel-le-Dale and my solo circuit finished there 5 hrs and 13 minutes later. It had been a lovely summer's day with little wind, and I dispensed with waterproofs and wore lightweight running shoes in place of the boots that I'd thought, correctly, had been essential for the earlier rounds in November 1978 and November 1979. I ran a solo round again in 1983 three minutes faster.

Here I must take issue with the great Alfred Wainwright who, in his introduction to his description of the Three Peaks Walks, writes '*Inevitably, and regrettably, it has become the subject of competitive races...*' I cannot accept his regretting, for I doubt if he ever experienced the sheer joy of fast movement over difficult terrain. If he had, he would understand that running can produce an uplifting sense of well-being without the serious damage caused by mind-altering drugs. Only those who have felt the wind in their hair and cooling their face on a hot day owing to the speed of their passage can understand the euphoria. They say that it's due to the production of natural endorphins that dull any pain. Anyone can become addicted because it costs nothing, it's good for your health and you may take a rest whenever you feel like it.

115

Taking a rest after running off PenyGhent
October 2nd 1996

THE LAKE DISTRICT 3,000s

I had intended to call this chapter "Long Walks" but soon realised that to do so would be confusing for readers expecting to find an account of The Pennine Way, Offa's Dyke or Mr. Wainwright's Coast to Coast walk. Those walks, and others of their ilk, are not merely long walks, they are long <u>distance</u> walks, and most walkers take several days to complete them. Here, I am concerned with a walk that may be completed within a single day.

There are many long walks (or runs) of which undoubtedly the best known is "The Bob Graham" (B.G. for short). In 1932, Bob Graham was a very fit guest house proprietor in Keswick, aged 42. He wondered how many of the mountains in the area he could cover in 24 hours, perhaps because he was aware that others had already covered what were then thought to be immense distances. One such was a Dr Wakefield, also of Keswick, who completed a circuit in 1904 that closely resembles a modern B.G. round. Despite having sprained a knee descending Yewbarrow, the good doctor finished in a little over 22 hours.

Bob Graham extended Wakefield's route to include 42 peaks, supposedly because that was his age in years. He covered 72 miles with 27,000 ft of climbing inside 24 hours. His record would stand for the next 28 years and although it became a standard route, it would be 1960 before his time was lowered by Alan Heaton and Stanley Bradshaw. It was almost inevitable that, as running shoe design improved and better and more serious training regimes developed, others would attempt to lower the record time still further. Also, it was not surprising that these exceptional athletes should set up a club for anyone completing the well-established round in under 24 hours. Harry Griffin in his booklet *42 Peaks – The Story of the Bob Graham Round*, records that at the end of 1981 there were 212 members. Today, at the end of 2020 there are 2,468.

But I am not writing this for such supermen. I never had any illusions. I was never to be a member of that distinguished

117

company, although I can say that I could have completed a B.G. round in under 24 hours by stitching together three separate walks, completed when time and opportunity allowed. Following a clockwise route, the first of these was from Keswick to Dunmail Raise which I walked and ran with three friends in 1986; the second stretch, from Dunmail Raise to Wasdale Head I did with Kathryn a year later in terrible weather (described later in Box of Delights 8). By then the cumulative time was 15 hours and 35 minutes so I had about eight and a half hours left. But I never finished the self-imposed task, partly because I left the UK to work in India.

The remaining time, however, was well inside my proposed schedule, so on my return I split the final leg into two sections – Wasdale Head to Honister, and Honister to Keswick, both of which I did alone, as and when the opportunity arose and inside the remaining time.

I knew I'd begun too late in life to take my fitness seriously, but I was happy enough to climb a mountain or two and take my time over it, accepting that I would soon get out of breath if I pushed myself a little. I only learned too late that if I had been fitter, I could have enjoyed myself even more and walked much further, and with no more than mild discomfort.

For we lesser mortals there was the easier challenge of the four Lake District "Three Thousands" – Scafell, Scafell Pike, Helvellyn and Skiddaw, all over three thousand feet, to be completed in a day. The minimum distance is 46 miles and the height to be climbed is about 11,000 ft. For many years the Ramblers Association has organised an annual event, usually in June to make use of the longer daylight hours. There are ten check points that walkers must visit and the Association provides refreshments at Seathwaite in Borrowdale and at Steel End by Thirlmere. Twenty-two hours are allowed to complete the circuit.

I had no doubts about my ability to complete the circuit in the given time but, apart from fell races, I am not partial to events that involve crowds of people, even though, after a mass start, as I have recorded elsewhere, the entrants are often soon strung out. I would much rather set off either alone or with a few friends of similar ability and enjoy a walk mostly uncluttered by a need to register my presence at several pre-set locations. Such a restriction for me is an imposition that I don't need, even though I might pass through that location anyway. This is not to decry the Ramblers Association in any way though, because it's an organisation of which I strongly approve with its many campaigns for access to the countryside, to wild places and the "Right to Roam". It was founded in 1935, two years before I was born, due in part to events such as the Kinder Scout Mass Trespass of 1932, reinforced by growing unrest amongst the general public, many of whom were seeking an escape from the daily drudgery of their working lives.

My first attempt was on Saturday, September 11th 1981, with three of my work colleagues who had previously, though not all together, accompanied me at times on the Yorkshire three peaks. Brian, Pat and Stuart, like myself, were all reasonably fit, though less familiar with the area and also perhaps not quite as enthusiastic. Brenda and I booked into a B&B in Keswick so Brenda would be free to do as she wished until I returned. Because I'd arranged to meet the others at Keswick Moot Hall for a midnight start, I explained to our hostess that I would be leaving that evening and return the following day. The reason for the late start was so that we could be up and down Skiddaw in darkness, so allowing us to climb the more dangerous mountains in daylight. This was just as well because by 4.00 am we had done with Skiddaw and were walking the length of Borrowdale four abreast in total darkness. And yes! I mean total darkness. I had no idea who was next to me unless someone spoke, and I had to ask who was eating an orange when I sensed it by the smell. Torrential rain began before we reached Rosthwaite, by which time dawn was breaking.

By Seathwaite the rain had eased a little and it was time for breakfast, but we stayed there a little longer than I'd hoped when Pat decided to attend to his usual morning ablutions by washing himself and cleaning his teeth. The weather had improved as we knocked off the Scafells, but by the time we reached Wythburn, we had started to slow down and the 35 mile and 8,000 ft that we'd covered had taken us 16 hours. Brian and Pat both had appointments to keep and needed to drive home so they decided to retire. Stuart and I, although capable of continuing, also thought it best to abandon the attempt. As I had come to expect, on the following day, the ankle that I'd damaged on the Outward Bound course was extremely painful – a condition that I had come to know would always be the same after a long walk or a marathon.

A year later, in July 1982, Brenda attended a four-day NHS conference at Lady Margaret Hall college in Oxford, so I took the opportunity to try for another round of the 3,000s, this time with Brian. The arrangements this time were that we would camp at Seatoller and set off earlier at 9.30 pm. Brian's son drove us to Keswick where we had a good meal of French onion soup at the Dog and Gun before starting off to climb Skiddaw taking the path through Fitz Park to Spooney Green Lane and the bridge over the A66 that we'd used the previous year. Soon after turning from the top of Gale Road on to the fell, there is a monument to men of the Howell family of Lonsdale that bears the legend – *Great Shepherd of Thy heavenly flock/These men have left our hill./ Their feet were on the living rock,/Oh guide and bless them still.* It's an easy place to find in the dark so we left our packs there to be collected on our descent.

We were soon over Skiddaw and being early July, the night sky never really darkened as much as it had done in 1981. Nevertheless, rain began again as we walked the length of Borrowdale and we were thankful for our tents at Seatoller where we spent three hours waiting for it to ease off. That rest wasn't really necessary but there seemed to be no point in walking in the rain, and we had ample time to complete the round in daylight. My bad ankle began to seize up but once we set off again it loosened up and gave me no further trouble. Although the rain had stopped, we were in cloud before we reached Styhead. It persisted until we reached Angle Tarn after negotiating the Scafells. Despite the enveloping clouds, I managed to negotiate the route correctly and was particularly proud of finding the bottom of Lord's Rake spot on by compass with no

120

landmarks as a guide. The sun came out to watch us as we traversed the slopes of Rossett Pike to the top of the Stake Pass. From there the distances seemed to be shorter and the Wythburn valley, despite the earlier rain, was drier than I had ever known it.

Helvellyn, the last summit, was as steep as ever but on reaching the top, knowing that we had only a long trudge back along the road, I produced two cans of lager from my haversack to celebrate. Those we enjoyed as we crossed Helvellyn's Lower Man in glorious sunshine to descend to the road at Thirlspot and the road to Keswick. We had dinner that night at the Yew Tree in Seatoller, both of us trying with difficulty not to fall asleep before returning to the tent. If we hadn't spent three hours waiting for the rain to stop at Seatoller, we would have been round in 18 hours – a most satisfying time.

My second successful circuit was in June 1985 with the same Pat who had insisted on cleaning his teeth after breakfast on the first, failed attempt four years earlier. This time, logistics dictated that we start from Wythburn and climb Helvellyn first. Rather than carry our packs all the way, before parking the car behind Wythburn church, I drove along the Keswick Road to a point where we could leave the packs behind a wall to be retrieved later. Whether you look on this as cheating, I leave it to you to decide. This wasn't a competition so why not make life as easy as possible on an otherwise unsupported walk.

We left the car park at 7.15 pm and were on Helvellyn's summit 55 minutes later. We were running well and, feeling confident, I decided to follow the Bob Graham route as far as possible going anti-clockwise to add a little more distance. We stayed on the ridge as far as the Sticks Pass from where we ran very fast down to the Keswick Road to collect our packs. That was my undoing for once on the road I knew I had blisters on the soles of both feet. The next 40 plus miles would be sheer hell. There was no need to walk into Keswick as far as Spooney Green Lane because I'd checked that we could cross the river Greta at a point almost directly below the newly built Keswick by-pass. From there we could climb Latrigg directly by following a fire-break through the forestry plantation.

This we did, even though it would add a little extra height to the standard round. At the foot of Latrigg, wanting to ease my painful feet, I suggested to Pat that he might like to climb Skiddaw alone and I would wait for him at the Moot Hall in Keswick. He refused point blank, which I suppose in retrospect and in view of the fading light, was the correct decision.

We left our packs by the Howell monument as Brian and I had done and continued by torchlight whenever we thought it necessary. We passed many ghostly torch-lit travellers as we climbed and there was an eerie stillness despite the gale force winds that we met on the summit. We felt sorry for a Clayton runner who, we'd been told, was attempting a Bob Graham round that day.

Pat had heard about, but never seen, the Bowder Stone and dawn was breaking as we approached Rosthwaite, so I took him on a short detour before we reached Seathwaite at 6.15 am. Soon afterwards rain set in for the rest of the day, which in one way was a blessing because I was still suffering from the blisters and the rain soon penetrated my running shoes to act as both a lubricant and a coolant. Nevertheless, at Styhead I suggested to Pat for a second time that he could climb Scafell and the Pike. I would walk directly to the shelter on Esk Hause and wait for him there. He'd been that way three years earlier and should have had no trouble with route finding but again he demurred. After some serious thought I had to agree with him as I remembered how a single visit to Scafell Pike had not been enough for me to be sure of my surroundings way back in 1957.

The Scafells were by now a familiar area for me and I'd had no problem two years earlier, so once again I gritted my teeth and set off along the Corridor route. At the foot of Lord's Rake I tried again to persuade Pat to allow me to omit the mountain, but was met again by a refusal so I took him up the West Wall traverse, the same way that I'd led Brian, and we descended by the same path. By then, every step was agonising and I was getting slower and slower as I tried to plant my feet in the least painful way possible on the rocky ground between the Scafells and Esk Hause. We were now

122

being sustained by chocolate raisins, "Sportscraft" drinks and Crunchies, but at least I told myself, every step was one step nearer the finish.

As we approached Esk Hause, a lone runner appeared out of the mist, coming up from somewhere that we guessed would be Borrowdale. He must have been surprised to see us because he stopped for a quick chat and we recognised Billy Bland, one of my fell running heroes, who was out on a training run. Despite the rain, he was dressed in only a singlet and shorts, so we didn't detain him long. The mist never lifted as we passed Angle Tarn and then took the familiar path contouring around Rossett Pike to the Stake Pass.

The climb over Raise seemed interminable and I suspect, although I'll never know for certain, that at one point I made a navigational error. I'd had the compass out since Scafell Pike and had referred to it frequently, but in the thick mist, there loomed up suddenly above us an immense crag (or so it seemed), which I think could only have been Sergeant Man. We passed below it and I continued with Pat a few yards behind me. For mile after mile, I could sense the unspoken daggers in my back until he asked, not surprisingly, 'Do you know where we are?' to which I had to give an honest reply, 'No, I don't, but I know which way we're going.'

Shortly after that, we dropped out of the mist to see the head of the Wythburn valley directly below us. For how long we'd been following a line parallel to the correct path (if there is one) I've no idea, but I'm glad Pat has forgiven me, although he hasn't let me forget*. We were back at the car by 3.30 pm after a walk that lasted for 20 hours and 15 minutes. I drove us home thankful that I didn't need to use the gear change pedal too much.

~~~~~

*Note: I wrote this in early 2021. Much to my regret, my friend Pat died on March 5th 2022 so I can now write that he forgave me but never let me forget. I attended his funeral together with Brian, who accompanied me on my other successful circuit of the Lake District 3,000s.

WELSH WALKS

There are fourteen 3,000 ft mountains in Wales compared to a mere four in the English Lake District. Not only that, but they are also more rugged and less forgiving to anyone who fails to respect the homage due to them. On the other hand, they are all confined within a smaller area than those of the Lake District. Consequently, the horizontal distance required to climb them all is much shorter although the total ascent is greater. Unlike the Lake District round though, the Welsh 3,000s challenge doesn't complete a circuit that ends at the starting point. It starts on any chosen summit and ends on the summit of the fourteenth (some say fifteenth, or even sixteenth) having visited all the others *en route,* so it is difficult to make any sort of meaningful comparison.

As with most such "challenges", the origin of the walk is shrouded in mystery although Thomas Firbank in his book *I Bought a Mountain* devotes a whole chapter to it. He started from Snowdon summit and finished on Foel Fras 8 hours and 25 minutes later, effectively pioneering what has since become the most frequented route.

By 1985, I had twice completed the Lake District 3,000s so it seemed a logical progression to attempt the Welsh equivalent. I was already familiar with much of the terrain but there were long stretches that would be new to me. Of course, the first thing I did was to study the map. This would have been unnecessary had I wanted only to set foot on each of the summits – the route was by then well documented, but that didn't really appeal to me after the Lake District rounds. It seemed to me that it wasn't quite kosher to finish at a place different from where I started. I began to look for alternative routes between summits, trying to find the shortest, easiest route that would involve the least expenditure of energy. This involved many hours poring over maps, plotting charts, measuring distances, checking heights and calculating times, but try as I might, the logistics eventually proved too much.

The major problem with trying to design a round trip is the configuration of the landscape that confines those Welsh mountains

124

into three major groups – the Carneddau, the Glyderau and the Snowdon massif. There was clearly no simple return route from Foel Fras at the north end of the Carnedd range (where Thomas Firbank finished) other than returning by the outward route to Ogwen, from where there were at least two alternatives back to Snowdon summit, assuming that had been the starting point. I even considered starting from Pen-y-Pass or Ogwen, but again, there was little to commend either as a starting point and eventually I shelved the idea for someone younger and with more energy and enthusiasm to complete. The additional height and distance were transforming the challenge to something approaching a Bob Graham round rather than a simple walk in one direction.

But my assiduous attention to the map would bear some fruit. Ten years later, approaching my 60th birthday, Brenda wanted to take her younger brother (another David) on the Snowdon Mountain railway, so I arranged to accompany them to North Wales. It would give me an ideal opportunity for a day on the Welsh hills. For many years I'd had a desire to add the Carneddau summits to my list of ascents so I suggested to Brenda that she could drop me off at Aber Falls, close to the coast road, and we could meet in the late afternoon in Llanberis at the mountain railway terminus. This would give me quite long enough, let's say about 5 or 6 hours to traverse the Carneddau range as far as Llyn Ogwen. From there, depending on how I felt, I could continue to Llanberis either by climbing one or more of the Glyderau or crossing the ridge to the Llanberis Valley using the Twll Du (Devils' Kitchen) path.

The weather was not auspicious when Brenda left me at the Aber Falls car park, but it was a warm September day and my calculations, using my own variations to Naismith's formula, gave me ample time to reach Llanberis by 5.00 pm. My version of the formula equates an ascent of 1,000 ft to two miles of level walking and the time for a walk is then calculated by simply assuming a walking pace of three miles per hour.

Perhaps because there was likely to be rain later on that September Wednesday, there were few cars on the car park and I met nobody all day until I dropped down to Llyn Ogwen. When I left the Aber Falls car park, I followed the valley road to its end. From that point I made a slight diversion up the steep slope to my right. I estimated the cloud base to be about 2,000 ft. but enough of the lower slopes was visible to allow me to make an informed guess as to where I wanted to be heading. In any case, knowing that I would be going off the map, I was carrying my compass but no map because a map for half the walk seemed superfluous. I had memorised as much of the route as I needed.

I must add here that I do not recommend that others should do the same unless they have confidence in their own judgement. There is always the chance of having an accident or meeting unexpected problems, or even becoming irretrievably lost. In my own defence I would add that Brenda always knew where I was going and would contact the emergency services should I fail to turn up by an arranged time (plus agreed extra time). Also, I had then over forty years of experience behind me during which I had developed what I suppose is a sixth sense of how landscapes have been moulded by time and the weather, of why the earth below your feet slopes the way it does, of why the wind is blowing from a particular quarter, or how a distant hillside disappearing into cloud will change direction inside that cloud. This of course will depend primarily on knowing exactly where you are at any given moment, what you can recall of the map (assuming you've not bothered to take it with you) and what your compass is telling you.

On this day, I knew that I would need to keep a line of electricity pylons that crossed the range from west to east to my left, while to my right would be the deep valley that held the Afon Anafon leading up to Llyn Anafon. Consequently, navigation was no problem, and I followed the crest of a ridge that led me unerringly to the summit of Drum (Carnedd Penyddorth-goch). For the last couple of miles or so I'd been in cloud but, remembering past indiscretions, I had kept my compass available all the way and knew that I should now be heading a little west of due south to Foel Fras, which I reached in under two hours, still in mist. It was now a simple matter of following the ridge from summit to summit, although under the prevailing conditions I elected to omit the diversion from Carnedd Llewelyn to Yr Elen and back. At that point I was becoming aware that I was no longer a (reasonably) fit middle-aged fell runner and I couldn't afford to be late at my Llanberis rendezvous.

It was perhaps as well that I eschewed the detour to Yr Elen because the decent to Llyn Ogwen down the abominable steep screes and shattered rocks of Pen yr Ole Wen took me far longer than I had budgeted for. Moreover, a thin persistent drizzle that lasted for the remainder of the day had set in, necessitating me to don my waterproof top.

Because I was moving relatively fast, I could keep warm easily enough and, in any case, I have always preferred wet legs to wet trousers. I paid for a welcome mug of hot sweet tea at Ogwen and checked the time. I had two hours left to reach Llanberis without causing a family row and, noting that the cloud base was now much lower than when I left Aber Falls, it was clear that I would have to use the Twll Du path across the ridge to the Llanberis Valley rather than include an ascent of another mountain.

The dismal trudge across the sodden plateau between Glyder Fawr and Y Garn was a disappointing end to what until then had been a stimulating exploration of new ground. My only regret was that the whole traverse of the Carneddau had been in mist with never a sight of the glorious views that should have been available to me. I had no need to hurry down the Llanberis road and I reached the rail station well before the rendezvous time. Brenda and David turned up soon afterwards having had a good day with better weather on Snowdon.

If Cadair Idris were seventy feet higher, it would be counted amongst the 3,000s and so would have extended the Welsh 3,000s "challenge" considerably. It's a pity that it falls short and is excluded from that august company of Snowdonia peaks because it's a worthy mountain in its own right. Basically, Cadair Idris (true name Penygadair) is a ridge that extends roughly from north-east to south-west for about twelve miles without a road crossing. Both ends of the ridge are of little interest to the serious mountain climber, but the central section is bounded by impressive crags that enclose Llyn y Gadair to the north and Llyn Cau to the south. The nearest town to Cadair Idris of any size is Dolgellau and that is where Brenda and I decided to spend a few days in March 1995.

Many years before, in 1958, we had spent two weeks on holiday at Harlech before we were married. From there, we had used the local train to get to Dolgellau to do the "Precipice Walk". My guidebook told me that this walk was much loved by Victorians with a taste for adventure during the golden days of rail travel. I was no different, for the name was the major attraction. But the walk itself I thought was a disappointment. It was not at all anything that resembled my idea of a precipice, although admittedly the walk followed a horizontal path on a very steep slope high above a valley that contained a constant stream of traffic. In later years I began to wonder if we had really followed the walk described in the guidebook. But I returned recently in 2019, much better informed, using the Ordnance Survey Outdoor Leisure map 23 that had not been available in 1958. This time I was able to drive up from Dolgellau to the start of the walk and confirm that we had indeed done the walk. My evidence was a photograph of distant hills that matched those in one that I'd taken of Brenda as she walked the path some sixty years previously. The views westward, out towards the Mawddach estuary were well worth the walk. For our earlier walk we'd begun with an uphill road walk from the town and back to catch the return train to Harlech.

Now, several years later, we elected to spend a day walking by the river and then around the Cregennan lakes, a little-known area but one of great beauty. The following day I had Cadair Idris in my sights, but Brenda wanted a nostalgic return to Harlech, so we compromised. After breakfast, she would drive me to Ty-nant from where I would run/walk up the Pony track and descend using the Foxes track to meet her at the hotel at mid-day. Both paths are well-documented. Although it was late March, it was a lovely day with scarcely a cloud in the sky and a gentle breeze was blowing off the coast to the south-west. There were a few small patches of snow still lying in shadow and also close to the summit shelter. I wished later

128

that I'd taken my camera, but I was travelling light with as few encumbrances as possible and I was back at the hotel well inside my predicted time. My first visit had been too hasty. I should have lingered on the top long enough to savour the views and enjoy the solitude, for I encountered no one. I vowed to return before too long.

But there was more to come that day before we returned home. The weather at sea level was set fair and we'd enjoyed strolling round Harlech remembering our exploits almost forty years earlier. We (that is, I) decided to return home by driving to Betws-y-Coed by way of Snowdon. Brenda agreed to drop me off in Nant Gwynant at the start of the popular Watkin path from where I would climb Snowdon. She would then drive round to Llanberis to take the train to the summit where we would meet for coffee in the café. Snowdon's summit is out of sight where the path starts, so neither of us had any idea of the state of the upper slopes. I only realised that the summit was still covered in snow when I turned the corner of a hillside about thirty minutes later – by which time Brenda would be near Llanberis, if not already there. There was nothing for it but to carry on without worrying, even though the thought crossed my mind that much higher up it would be much colder than at sea level.

As usual, I was travelling light, and with a clear, cloudless sky there was no chance of bad weather. I confess I'd forgotten that the railway closes during the winter, usually until Easter, and because that festival was still three weeks away, I wasn't bothered about where and when we might meet.

I was moving fast enough to keep warm despite being lightly clad in my usual fell running gear and trainers, so even when I reached the snow line, probably at about 2,000 ft well below Bwlch Ciliau between Snowdon's summit and Y Lliwedd, I stayed warm despite having wet feet. The higher I climbed the deeper the snow became, but I was not the first to pass that way, so the path was easy enough to follow, although it soon became clear there would be no train at the top. Sure enough, close to the summit café, the rail tracks were lying beneath at least six feet of snow.

There was no point in hanging around getting cold, so I set off

129

to run down the line of the railway. Approaching Clogwyn station I heard the train ascending and I arrived there just as it pulled in and stopped, that being as far as it would go that day. As the passengers disembarked, I saw Brenda amongst them and ran down to embrace her in a hug that all the watching passengers probably thought must have been pre-arranged. From there, we walked together down to Llanberis in what was rapidly turning into a biting wind.

That same year, remembering my vow to return to Cadair Idris, we went again to Dolgellau in October on our way to the annual meeting of the Association of Methodist Scouters and Guiders (AMSAG). When we left after a couple of days easy walking in the area, I told Brenda I'd like to cross over the mountain and meet her on the roadside at the highest point on the A487 (a spot height, 285 metres) where Tal-y-llyn Lake comes into sight for anyone travelling towards it from the north-east. To do so would give me a chance to explore a side of the mountain I'd never seen.

Unfortunately, the cloud base was very low when I set off up the Foxes path and remained so until I reached the road at the end of my walk. I saw nothing that day beyond an ever-changing view of rocks and grass to either side of the path until I was a few hundred feet above the road. The arranged meeting point described above may have seemed a little hit and miss, but as I emerged from the mist to descend towards the road, I saw our car stop exactly where I expected. My navigation had been easy enough owing to there being a good track to follow as far as the summit, and then a single compass bearing check to meet up with a wall that led me unerringly down to the road.

My third and final ascent of Cadair Idris would be eleven years later in June 2006. Brenda was taking her younger brother, David, for a trip on the Tal-y-Llyn railway so naturally I hitched a lift again, this time as far as Minffordd, from where I could traverse the mountain while they took the train down to the coast at Tywyn and back again. We had arranged to meet later inside the café at Abergynolwyn station. Again, it was a day of rain when the clouds were trailing their muddy skirts along the valley floor and visibility was reduced to a circle of perhaps a twenty-metre radius. But such were the days that I relished then. Brenda thought I was mad, for those were the sort of days when skilful fishers would go not forth, and the madding crowds would all stay indoors.

I took with me a list of compass bearings and a roughly sketched map of where I wanted to be. Most of the route was new ground for me and the low cloud added a further hazard. At first the path was clear and distinct and, for someone approaching seventy years of age, I made good progress. From Minffordd, the path climbs to Llyn Cau which I knew to be surrounded by a magnificent semi-circular rocky combe. Beyond the lake, the path ascends steeply through the only break in those defences. (I have since learned that there are a number of other routes to the summit from that side of the ridge). Once I had reached the lake the path became less distinct, perhaps because the many tourists that climb so far to experience the grandeur of the scene decide that they may as well stop there. But I pressed on along the lake shore hoping to find an obvious point at which the upward path began. I came across no such point, so I had to assess where I was and use my judgement – had I gone too far or not far enough?

It was now a case of climbing through mist into the unknown. The lower slopes were relatively easy but little by little the gradient became ever steeper until, by knowing my rate of climbing, I considered that if I didn't reach the ridge soon, I would have to retreat. To do that would involve a long and tedious walk along the road – not an attractive proposition. So, with what seemed like near vertical rocks towering above me to right and left, it was time to rest, drink some water and eat some mint cake.

Suitably refreshed, I resumed the ascent and almost immediately found myself on the ridge where a westerly gale lashed me with horizontal rain. Five minutes later I was in the summit refuge sheltering from the gale. Was it luck or experience that led me there? I don't know but I like to think the latter. When I looked out from the shelter some minutes later, I saw the clouds being torn to shreds by the wind and it wasn't long before the sun was shining down from a clearing sky. Such was my reward for climbing into the unknown. The only blot on the landscape was a solitary walker heading up my proposed line of descent. We passed with a surly 'Hi!' and 'Hello', each of us knowing instinctively what the other was thinking: 'But for you I would have had this mountain to myself today.'

I reached Abergynolwyn station with plenty of time to find the car, change into dry clothes and enjoy a mug of hot sweet tea and a sandwich before the train arrived. 'Did you have a good day?' Brenda asked.

'Perfect,' I replied, 'How about you?' While adding to myself as I thought of that other walker, *Well, almost.*

I was also disappointed that I had seen nothing of the rocky slopes on either side of my climb and resolved that one day I would return, but fifteen years would pass before a suitable occasion would present itself. By July 2021, my circumstances had changed considerably. Brenda and her brother, David, had both died, Kathryn and Peter had migrated from New Zealand to Cyprus and the Covid-19 pandemic that began in 2020 was still raging, although restrictions were being relaxed.

I had no photographs of Cadair Idris and because I wanted one, I'd already decided to go as soon as the weather and circumstances were favourable. Rosalind and Adrian were to be married in July and Kathryn came with Peter to attend her sister's wedding. They quarantined with me during a period of hot weather that broke many records up and down the country. As soon as they were out of quarantine, I drove them to Minffordd, wanting no more than a photo of Llyn Cau. The drive from home takes two and a half hours so we set off before 6.00 am and were at the Minffordd car park at 8.15 am to begin the climb to the lake.

There were several cars already on the car park which surprised me, but when we met several people coming down, we learned that they had been up to watch the sunrise. Even so early, the heat was such that we had to refill our water bottles when we reached the lake. There, I took several photos, from which I could select the best, but the lure of the summit could not be ignored. Kathryn wanted to reach the summit, so she set off to run anti-clockwise along the lake shore while Peter and I followed much more slowly.

For most of the way, we could see her approaching the ridge, but we had to watch where we were placing our own feet on the rocky track and eventually she disappeared from sight. From the far end of the lake we began to climb up a steep slope of shattered scree that consisted mostly of slate-like stones that I didn't remember. Fortunately, we had crossed a substantial stream where we had re-filled out water bottles. The heat of the day had been steadily increasing and we were well below the ridge when we saw Kathryn returning. There, above a substantial outcrop of quartzite, we stopped to rest until she reached us.

Llyn Cau on Cadair Idris
The summit of Pen-y-Gadair is off the photo to the right.
July 21st 2021

I was still keen to reach the summit, but Kathryn was adamant that it would be not only beyond my ability, but also foolish and reckless. And with hindsight, and remembering the heat, I think I knew she was right. On such a hot day, that was not a country, and certainly not a mountain, for old men! We ate our lunch and descended back to the stream where, once again we needed to re-fill our water bottles. The walk back to the car, even though mostly downhill, was a test of perseverance. I had to stop several times to relieve the arthritic pain in my hips, not to mention that from the titanium implant in my left femur. By the time we reached the car park café, our water bottles were empty again. But it had been a day of wonderful scenery and stunning views.

BEN MACDUI

For the 1976 Easter holiday we took the girls to stay for a week in a guest house at Boat of Garten in the Spey Valley. The Wednesday coincided with Brenda's 39th birthday and the weather was hot and sunny. Earlier in the week we'd taken the chairlift to the Ptarmigan restaurant at the top of Cairngorm so that I could check out the feasibility of climbing Ben Macdui later in the week. After a family discussion we decided that, if the day after Brenda's birthday was fine, she would spend the day with Kathryn by Loch Morlich, while Rosalind would climb Ben Macdui with me.

Being in the homeland of Robbie Burns, I should have guessed that all my best laid plans would "gang aglae". Brenda had agreed to drive Rosalind and me up to the White Lady Shieling at the foot of the chair lift which we would then use to take us up to the Ptarmigan restaurant. From there we would begin our walk to Ben Macdui across the Cairngorm plateau. But sod's law (or perhaps Robbie Burns) intervened before we even started. There was not a cloud in the sky and Brenda had driven off with Kathryn before Rosalind and I learned that the chair lift was not operating that day. I still intended to climb Ben Macdui so this meant a change of plan, even though it would involve considerably more climbing. Despite the sweltering heat of the sun that had already lasted for the previous few days, several extensive snow fields were still lying on slopes where the snow had lain deepest. I doubt if we would have slipped but I had my ice axe with me and used it occasionally, though probably unnecessarily, as we traversed across a large snow field on the slopes of Coire Cas. We were heading towards a low point in the Cairngorm plateau and once there, we could see before us the deep and seemingly endless trough of Glen Avon with Ben Macdui somewhere beyond.

This was pathless country and I guess we climbed to a col at the head of Coire Raibert where we found a torrent of water issuing from beneath a small snowfield. We descended then by the side of the resulting stream, being very careful to watch where we placed

135

our feet on this trackless ground. When we reached the shore of Loch Avon, we turned right to follow the vestige of a path upstream noting that the rushing waters were swollen from melting snow. Because I'd been concentrating on safety during the descent, I'd not taken much notice of the scenery, so when I stopped for a moment to scan the forbidding face of the mountain on the far side of the valley, I thought it might be too much for us to climb with our limited equipment. Being in such a remote spot and aware of the consequences of an accident in such isolation I was by then secretly a little worried.

We spent some time searching up and down the stream for a suitably safe place to cross. One consolation was that we were able to visit the famous shelter stone about which I had read much. I understood then why it has that name. Although the rock face that towered above us had at first sight looked so daunting, now that we were much nearer, I was able to pick out a snow filled gully that I guessed would be safe enough to lead us back up to the plateau. The apparent steepness that I'd supposed earlier had obviously been caused by foreshortening.

However, I still thought it prudent to use the axe to cut steps in the frozen snow, but we had no rope to safeguard Rosalind. Fortunately, she had with her (again) a scarf, long enough to be tied around both our wrists to join us and so allow us to move upwards separately, while using the ice axe as a safety anchor.

Once we were on the plateau, the long walk on well-trodden snow to the summit of the Ben that followed was enlivened by one other case of serendipity when we almost trod on a mountain hare. It was still in its winter coat, so we hadn't noticed it until it went bounding away towards Glen Avon. We reached the summit without further incident and the rest of the day was an anti-climax. We had a long wearisome return walking across the plateau, eventually descending by the flanks of Cairn Lochan across another huge snowfield. We reached the road near the roadside car park for The Glen More Forest Park where we met Brenda and Kathryn. We were fifteen minutes later than my promise – the first and only time I have ever failed to keep a rendezvous on time.

Snow field in Coire Cas on the way to Ben Macdui
Easter 1976

THE LAIRIG GHRU

(Scotland, June 1983 and June 1993)

In June 1983, Brenda and I spent two weeks touring Scotland during which I had a few short days on the hills. One of these was the ascent of Ben Venue on a very hot day. I wore only a vest, shorts and running shoes and had taken a brief look at the map. Visibility was excellent so there was no danger of getting lost. I never even bothered to consider that I might encounter an unexpected obstacle. I told Brenda to expect me back in a couple of hours and to wait another 30 minutes before raising the alarm if I was late – my usual precaution. With no idea of the route, I set off from the shore of Loch Katrine through a trackless wilderness of knee-high bracken, bilberries and beech groves and was on the summit inside an hour.

I could have descended by the same mountainside but thought I'd take a bee line back to the bottom end of the lake through a forest of pine trees. This gave me the first unexpected obstacle for that day in the form of a deer fence surrounding the forest. To turn to either side would make me so late that Brenda would be calling the mountain rescue services out. I had no option but to find a stout post and climb over the fence, being careful not to cause any damage. I was soon back on track to keep to my schedule, but there was now a further problem.

In theory, if I continued to descend I would at some point reach the loch shore, but the trees were planted so closely together that their branches were intertwined and I couldn't pass through them while upright – I had to drop almost to my knees to pass under the lower branches, most of which were dried and withered owing to a lack of sunlight. Furthermore, it was such a steep slope that in places I had to resort to sliding on my backside on a carpet of dry pine needles.

When I spied what I thought was daylight from a clearing a couple of hundred or so yards ahead, I made directly for it, only to find that the absence of trees was because they ended on top of a sheer rock face. With great difficulty I managed to by-pass this and then by various routes, wherever the trees thinned out a little, I reached the loch shore and met Brenda with five minutes to spare inside my estimate, although with arms, legs and shoulders bleeding from a multitude of scratches.

The hot weather continued when we reached Fort William. From there Ben Nevis was an obvious target for me. Brenda drove to the car park in Glen Nevis near the youth hostel from where I began, having first bought a can of lemonade. Again, because this was during my fell-running years, I was wearing a vest, shorts and running shoes. Glen Nevis was shimmering in the heat of the morning. I was very hot, but the newly bought lemonade was ice cold. By the time I reached the summit an hour and 25 minutes later, I was beginning to feel cold, but the lemonade was hot from the heat of my sweaty hands.

Although I found the ascent by the mountain track very boring, I was impressed by the sheer bulk of the mountain and the crags of the North face, even seen from the edge of the plateau above, not to mention the care put into maintaining the easy tourist track. There were too many people on the summit to linger and the evidence of past human activity (the observatory ruins) disfigures the plateau. As soon as I had drunk the lemonade, I began my return intending to enjoy the lingering snowfields that I could use for glissading and I was down in 50 minutes.

The 3 Peaks Yacht race that takes in Snowdon, Scafell Pike and Ben Nevis was due to finish in Fort William that same day, so it was a delight, frequently to be asked if I was one of the entrants.

Moving on, we stopped in Aviemore where I saw that the Cairngorm fell race would be held the following day. I may have known this in advance from reading the FRA calendar and secretly arranged that we would be there in time for the event. I have never, before, or since, run in such a fell race where the marshals probably outnumbered the 33 competitors. Not only that, but the ten-mile route to the summit of Cairngorm and back was flagged every hundred yards or so – even on the road from the start to the finish!

There were prizes, donated by Lord Leven, to the first ten runners, the first veteran, and to the first three teams of three people. For once I was hoping I might win something as I tussled for a place with a white-haired elderly runner. I would pull away from him only to need to relax, so he would pass me until I put in a little more effort and regained the lead. On the descent as we crossed the car park at, I think, the lower ski lift station, my right knee became so painful that, try as much as I could, I had to watch him draw away from me and finish about 200 yards ahead. I learned later that he was Eddie Campbell one of the most famous Scottish fell runners of his era. In the early 1950s, while I was a teenager, he had won the Ben Nevis fell race three times. I still feel privileged to have run alongside such a runner.

But there was more to come, because Eddie Campbell was responsible for instigating the Lairig Ghru fell race, the first one being held on June 19th, 1976. That approximately 27 mile race began at Braemar police station and ended at Aviemore police station – and as far as I know, still does. The Lairig Ghru pass is the longest and one of the highest in the Scottish Highlands and a serious undertaking, even on a hot summer day. At nearly 2,740 ft the top of the pass is higher than Coniston Old Man and therefore also higher than most of the rest of the Lake District. Only experienced climbers should attempt to cross the pass in winter.

Lack of opportunity has precluded me from ever entering the race. Eddie Campbell produced a wonderful information sheet for the 1982 race. His sense of humour is clear from his statements that there would be NO changing rooms, NO numbers, NO recorder, NO starter, NO route markings, NO check points, NO rescue plans, NO first aid, NO transport etc. In other words, every entrant would be on his/her own from start to finish.

This was just the sort of run (not race) to appeal to me and I had a willing wife who would be happy to drop me off at Coylumbridge and be content to drive the sixty or so miles through Tomintoul to meet me at the Linn of Dee at the Braemar end, both of which would shorten the distance to about 20 miles. This fitted in with our plans to spend the next night on our way home at a B & B in Pitlochry.

So, at 9.30am on Monday June 27th,1983, two days after Eddie Campbell beat me in the Cairngorm fell race, Brenda dropped me off at Coylumbridge for one of the most enjoyable walks I have ever done. The first miles through the Rothiemurchus Forest were pure delight as I jogged along at an easy pace with the distant mountains gradually acquiring more detail as they emerged from occasional obscurity behind the Scots pines of the ancient Caledonian forest. Two miles into the walk I reached the Cairngorm Club footbridge where a sign informed me that the walk to the Linn of Dee would take me 8 hours. Because I'd allowed four hours and a half, this could have been discouraging, but because I wasn't walking but jogging, I had no worries and I pressed on after having a drink from the river. The path through the forest seemed to go on forever and I started to think how boring it might have been if I'd been walking, but eventually I emerged into open country that revealed a more expansive view of the grand mountains ahead and the pass that I would soon walk/run through.

Only two walkers that I passed were going my way; three more, who had spent the previous night in one of the mountain huts, were coming down. I would see nobody else until I reached Derry Lodge four miles from the end of my walk. I might have been the only person in the world when I reached the top of the pass in an hour and a half. There I found that snow was still lying amongst the shattered rocks fallen from Ben Macdui on my left and from Braeriach on my right. It was there that I disturbed a ptarmigan with a brood of newly hatched chicks that scurried away in fear of being trampled underfoot.

The view to the South-east now opened up and all but took my breath away. I could see no sign of habitation or anything at all that suggested the presence of human life. The path before me disappeared into the distance as far as I could see and, if I hadn't known that it takes a left turn about five miles further on, I might have thought that it would go on forever disappearing over the curve of the earth. But I had the map with me (although I never referred to it), and I knew that the path made a left turn into Glen Luibeg.

Gradually the path improved underfoot, and I seemed to have wings on my heels as I raced down from the pass without any effort towards the far off turning. I was aware of the Corrour bothy away to my right nestling below the Devil's Point, a shoulder of Cairn Toul. There was nobody about. I couldn't resist stopping several times to admire the grandeur of the mountain scene that was forever changing, but I still reached Derry Lodge three and a half hours after leaving Coylumbridge, and the Linn of Dee thirty minutes later where I met Brenda walking up the road towards me with Sam, our little mongrel terrier. The whole walk had lasted for only four hours leaving us with plenty of time to drive to Pitlochry and our B & B for the night.

Ten years later, being very familiar with Scotland's west coast, we decided that we ought to have a look at the east coast. This turned out to be five days of a rain-soaked journey driving from Edinburgh to Aberdeen. Not surprisingly we visited a succession of castles and grand houses before ending up (by chance?) at Boat of Garten in the Spey valley for two nights. Here was an opportunity for me to repeat the crossing of the Lairig Ghru when we left our B & B for home, and with Brenda's blessing I took it. Hoping to save a little time and distance I asked her to drop me off about a mile beyond Coylumbridge, but I hadn't taken into account that I would have to cross the River Luineag which was much wider than I'd expected. Nor was there a bridge, so I had to remove shoes and socks and wade across. Using the shorter route had saved me nothing in time.

Unlike my earlier crossing, this was a Sunday and there were far more people about which didn't please me, but close to the top of the pass I had the Pools of Dee to myself, and I met nobody for three miles either side where ptarmigan were still changing from winter to summer plumage. Being ten years older I was slower by 45 minutes and, owing to the crowded car park at Linn of Dee, I found Brenda waiting for me half a mile up the road.

A FEW ROCK CLIMBS

I've never had any aspirations to emulate Joe Brown or Don Whillans, arguably the first pair of post-war rock climbers to set up a host of first ascents on vertical or overhanging rock faces. Many famous names have followed in their hand and foot holds, perhaps the most famous British climber today being Chris Bonington. My heroes during my teenage years, for being the first to reach the summit of Mount Kenya, and their explorations of the Himalaya, were Eric Shipton and Bill Tilman. As an adolescent, I read everything I could get my hands on if it referred to mountains of any shape or form. But work and part time study, not to mention lack of transport and finance, precluded any hope of me getting away to do any serious climbing.

Anyway, I could pretend, and one day I took my life, and possibly my career, in my hands. Every day since I started work in the Westwood power station laboratory in Wigan, I walked past a flat roofed building (the ash-processing plant) and noticed that the fourth (or was it fifth) row of bricks in the walls were recessed, leaving an inch wide ledge that would be ideal for climbing. The building was no more than about thirty feet high, but the challenge haunted me until one day of thick fog (there have been no such fogs since the implementation of the Clean Air Act in 1963) I decided to climb it.

I'd already been on the roof to ensure there was a way off to obviate the need to climb down and the fog would hide me from any distant watcher. Expecting that it would take only a few seconds, I waited until I was sure no one would be passing close by and began. Within seconds, I was well above eye level and guessed that anybody passing by at that stage would be unlikely to look up. The vertical climb was as easy as I'd hoped, but I'd forgotten the overhanging coping stones on the top. I now had to lean backwards and with the fingers of one hand precariously holding on, I had to stretch an arm over the top, hoping that it would be long enough to allow me to hook my fingers on the far side of the coping stone. Fearless or foolhardy? Make up your own mind, but I wouldn't recommend anyone to do it without a top rope. Anyway, the building was demolished many years ago.

The Outward Bound course taught me a lot about rock climbing and eventually I bought a hundred foot length of nylon rope and three karabiners in the hope of someday getting away for some simple climbs. I cut enough from the rope to make three slings to go with the karabiners, so its final length was reduced to about eighty feet. But before then, I'd had an opportunity for more climbing in April 1959 when Brenda and I were on our honeymoon We were staying at the Borrowdale Hotel (probably my choice) at the foot of Shepherds Crag. Going into the bar one day with Brenda, I recognised one of the OBMS instructors who immediately invited me to join him and his friend for a few climbs on Shepherds Crag. Brenda knew exactly what I was thinking because I hesitated before I turned the offer down. Under the circumstances I'm sure I made the right decision to take her for an afternoon rowing on Derwentwater.

Meanwhile, I'd bought the Fell and Rock Climbing Club (FRCC) Guides to Borrowdale and to the Coniston Fells and was also reading a monthly magazine *The Climber*. I've retained the issue for June 1967 because it became particularly interesting to me on two counts. First, it included an article on long distance views, relevant because I would subsequently experience some remarkably long views myself, and secondly because it included a description of a rock climb – Troutdale Pinnacle that I would climb (as a second) myself three years later.

For the October 1967 half-term, I booked a week in a self-catering cottage at Thorneythwaite Farm near Seatoller for the whole family, including my mum and dad and my brother Peter. We agreed that we wouldn't all do the same thing every day, so one day I took Peter, then aged seventeen, to lead him on a couple of climbs on Shepherds Crag. We climbed Brown Slabs Arete and Little Chamonix, experiencing a little difficulty identifying the locations and routes of both, but not experiencing any danger. About half-way up "Little Cham", to use its nickname, I must have strayed on to either Bludgeon or Crescendo (two other climbs) because the rock didn't seem to fit the guide-book description. Anyway, another climber and his friend set me right.

Because I was using my 80 ft rope, at the top of "Little Cham" I had just enough rope to reach a tree to use as a belay to safeguard Peter on the final pitch. The following day I intended taking Peter to climb Napes Needle. It was an inauspicious day as we set off. All that day the cloud level was low, and we hardly saw proper daylight. As we approached Sty Head, suddenly all the fiends of heaven were loosed upon us. Fury of furies.

Napes Needle
October 1967

Within seconds we turned our backs to the storm that raged through Sty Head. We raised our anorak hoods, donned plastic macs, retired behind a convenient boulder and let the storm rage about us only inches above our heads. Borrowdale was totally obscured, and we saw a couple of walkers that we had passed a few minutes earlier beating a hasty retreat before the onslaught. We stayed where we were and followed the progress of the storm by watching Styhead Tarn as gusts of wind and rain ruffled the surface, crossing it from side to side in seconds while whipping up flying sheets of spray.

Although I'd taken the rope, the conditions were such that no opportunity presented itself for us to use it on the Napes ridges or elsewhere. Once the wind and rain had eased, we left our sanctuary to scramble around the Gable Traverse as far as the Sphinx Rock from where we reached Gable's summit by way of the Westmorland cairn. We returned over Green Gable and Base Brown to Seathwaite. Meanwhile, the rest of the family had motored to Watendlath. There would be no chance of any more rock-climbing that year because a week later, the Great Foot and Mouth epidemic of 1967 began, and the fells were barred to walkers and climbers until the following February.

In June 1970, Brenda and I took our younger daughter, Kathryn, to stay for five nights at Barrow House Youth Hostel in Borrowdale while Rosalind was at school camp. It was a very hot week, and we swam a lot in Derwentwater and splashed about in the Churn at Watendlath. This is a delightful place on a hot day to scramble up easy rocks wearing a swimming costume alongside (or in) a tumbling waterfall. I'd taken the rope and one day I took Kathryn to Brown Slabs where we did two climbs – the Ordinary and the Direct.

The next day we were enjoying the hot sun, lying on the grass by the River Derwent at Grange, when a man who was leaning over the bridge noticed the rope beside me. He told us that the day before, he'd been frustrated following a slow party taking four hours to climb Troutdale Pinnacle. He then asked if I was a rock climber and on learning that I did a little, he asked me if I would like to accompany him on a repeat ascent. Brenda sensed my desire and said that she didn't mind, and might take Kathryn for a sail on

Derwentwater, so I accepted his offer to meet him the following day.

As I walked along the Borrowdale Road with George (for that was his name) to the turning into the charming, secluded Troutdale Valley, he warned me about a decomposing dead sheep at the foot of the climb and told me that we would soon be high enough to leave the disgusting smell below us. He was surprised to find me wearing heavy vibram soled boots, made for walking rather than climbing, and not the sticky rubber soled shoes that were coming into fashion at the time.

I knew nothing about George, and he knew nothing about me, so it was a matter of faith that we trusted each other. George must have worked out in advance who would lead each pitch because he asked me to lead the first one. Then, by alternating the pitches we would be able to climb more quickly. I didn't begin too well because I took some time getting accustomed to my contact with the unfamiliar rocks and the world being vertical instead of horizontal. This was a more serious undertaking than climbing the easier rocks of Brown Slabs up which I'd taken Kathryn two days before.

Probably George was thinking at that stage that he'd made a terrible mistake by inviting me. Anyway, I soon remembered techniques learned on the Outward Bound course and hand-jammed and wedged my way up the first crack, finding the way a lot easier thereafter. George soon followed and climbed through to the top of the next pitch. We carried on alternating the pitches in this way until we reached the pitch known (by me anyway) as "The Slab".

That was (and is) a sensational place to be. For non-climbers you must imagine you are standing on top of a roof that slopes below you almost vertically. If you look down you can't see anything beyond the lower edge of the roof until your eyes come to rest on trees and fields far away in the Troutdale valley bottom, hundreds of feet below – and you know there is nothing else below the slab except empty space.

It was at this point that George said that he would lead, and when I came to cross the slab myself, I realised why George had been so insistent on leading. When he was safely belayed, I began the traverse and saw that he'd put in a couple of runners to protect me if I slipped. I was thankful for them, even though I had no trouble with traversing the slab because the hand and foot holds were large and conveniently placed. However, there was a bulging rock to climb at the far end of the slab that reminded me of the coping stones that I mentioned earlier, soon after I began work. With George now belaying himself above me I had no trouble with the final tremendous finish and suddenly the climb was over. We'd climbed it in fifty-five minutes, and I wished it could have gone on forever. I later used the experience to write the short story *The Crux* that follows in the next chapter.

For the 1975 October half-term holiday, Rosalind joined a party staying at Loggerheads in North Wales. Brenda and I took Kathryn to Ambleside Youth Hostel for the weekend, and I took my copy of the Langdale FRCC (Fell and Rock Climbing Club) Guide to Langdale. Brenda was happy enough to drop Kathryn and me off at the New Dungeon Ghyll and drive herself back to Ambleside, while I took Kathryn to explore the crags of Pavey Ark. I'd looked through the guide for something that looked easy enough and settled on Cook's Tour because the description gave me the impression that it wandered from side to side as it ascended across the face of the crag rather than making straight for the top.

The climb begins perhaps a third of the way up Jack's Rake and didn't present any problems until Kathryn found that she couldn't stretch far enough across a traverse to reach a hold. We'd climbed far enough, so I decided that a retreat was called for. We had no problem descending the few pitches that we'd climbed from Jack's Rake and carried on to Gwynne's Chimney, which I remembered reading about in Gwen Moffatt's book *Space Below My Feet*.

I climbed the first pitch and belayed on for Kathryn to follow, but she was carrying a haversack which, because the chimney is constricted in places, gave her trouble with her balance. We solved the problem by Kathryn untying herself so that I could haul the haversack up first. I then threw the end of the rope down so that Kathryn could tie herself on as I'd taught her. There were no further problems and we continued to the summit still tied together although we were on much easier and safer ground.

THE CRUX

'Take in Slack.'
   'Taking in.'
   'That's me.'
   'Climb when you're ready.'
   'Climbing.'

East buttress. The familiar routine. Good to be on a rope again, blue sky above, green fields below, yellow lichen dappling the rock. A distant view of azure hills, range upon range. Study the rock. So close you feel a part of it. Crystals of quartz, feldspar, mica flash upon your eye. Let your eye wander over the face of the crag to where a million frosts have split the shear planes so that they shine like a mirror. Search for the damage when the earth eased itself from sleep, the cracks that allow you to climb, the cracks for the pitons that you hammer hard into the rock so that it moulds and holds them to its heart. The cracks that will scuff your fingertips and break your nails. Then caress its other face. The tortured roughened slabs. Roughnesses that give you friction holds as your hand glides slowly, ever so slowly, feeling your balance shifting gently, ever so gently to the side. Reaching and stretching. A single rowan tree struggles for survival. Exposed. Braving winter gales with limbs stretched outward and upward. Just you – and the tree – and the rope above, soaring up to heaven.

Then you move a foot.

Look down between your feet. Look at the scree, perhaps three hundred feet below. There's a dead sheep there that smelled so foul that you wanted to vomit. A falling stone would land beside it and come to rest. So would any falling body. Your body.

'What the hell are you doing down there?'

For God's sake shut up, Tom.

'Climbing'

'Well, don't take all bloody day. Where are you?'

'Climbing out of the coffin.' A lie.

'You mean the sentry box – that's what the guide-books call it.'

150

Stupid name for a stance, but descriptive. Move your foot again. Remember last time. Surely it wasn't so hard. Lean out sideways. Round a jagged corner of rock. Arm stretched, taut as your mind. Feel only smooth rock. Tilt you head back. Concentrate on balance. Feel it. Hold it. An inch at a time. At last. Fingers into the crack you were searching for. Flex them for the friction. Scrabble with your foot for the flake of rock you know is there, but you can't see. Transfer your weight. Rest.

The crack slants up now by the side of the bulging rock above the coffin (or the roof) of the sentry box. Take your pick. A delicate rising traverse with nothing but space below – until you land on the sheep. Reach one of Tom's pitons. Release the rope. Retrieve the piton for another day. Climb to the next. Good to have Tom above. An old campaigner. Good man on a rope. You can see him now. So he's going to be watching you. So you try to relax. Forget the pain. Make it look easy. Reach the belay. Tie yourself on.

'You took your time.'

'So would you after a year in a sick bed.'

'Sorry, I'd forgotten. You should have said. No fun on your own, is it?'

What does he mean by that last remark? Does he know something? Has Sandra let something slip? Get his mind back to climbing.

'Forget it. I'm belayed. Climb when you're ready.'

'Give me some slack then.'

Tom moves with the grace of a ballet dancer. An easy fluid motion. Hands and feet always in the right place. As if he were climbing a ladder. No hesitation. No mistakes. Tom won't fall. Never has. Turn away from the rock. Admire the view. What a stance – what a day. Trace the cloud shadows drifting over the swell of the fields. Like that day on Monte Rosa. The magic of the Dolomites. Do you remember an inn, Miranda? No, not in the high Pyrenees, and anyway her name was Sandra – Tom's wife. Remember wandering through the fields to the pretty village and the bar that you all used. Staggering back to the tents. Drinking at night – climbing by day. You had a skinful that time. Should never

151

have set off up Monte Pelmo. Lucky to fall before you'd gone too high. Lucky your back wasn't broken for good. Even luckier to have Sandra stay with you while Tom went off with Jack. They did the Civetta Direttissima and came back talking of nothing else for days.

After that, the big walls of the Marmolada. Tom and Jack climbing every day leaving you at a loose end with Sandra. Ironic really to dislocate your back while horizontal.

'More slack. You gone to sleep or something?' Tom's out of sight again, somewhere beyond the huge overhang above. The crux. No point looking up. No point in replying. Just wonder – what does he know? Why did he give you a bell yesterday? Does he know it's exactly a year to the day you were admitted to the hospital in Cortina d'Ampezzo? Another shout. Give him more rope. If Tom fell now, you'd have no chance. You couldn't hold him. Not with your back.

Tom flashes past. A graceful parabolic dive into space, the rope arcing behind in slow motion as the pitons spring out – ping, ping, ping. Watch the rope straighten and lengthen interminably, vibrating like a violin string. Wait to feel the weight and prepare yourself to fly. Don't even think about it. Shake yourself back to reality. Tom's shout disturbs you.

'Climb when you're ready.' What, so soon?

'Climbing.' But you hesitate. Why did Tom suggest we climb "Eliminate One"? He couldn't possibly mean to...

'What's up, lost your nerve or something?'

Lie again. 'No. Out of practice. Give me a tight rope.'

'Wilco.'

Well, there's no going back. Lean away from the rock and tilt your head back to search for holds. Your vertebrae compress and the pain starts. Not a glimmer of a hold. But Tom climbed it, there must be. Stretch to one side and let your fingers do the walking out of sight on the far side of a shallow rib. Find a scratch, enough to support two fingertips – if only your feet can find some friction. Move one foot. You've stopped breathing but you don't know. Far away a lamb bleats. Was that its mother lying dead below you?

152

Slowly transfer your weight to the side. Bring the other foot across. Relax and rest. Now the overhang. Reach up. Find a wrinkle. Pray that your arm strength will still be enough. Forget about Tom. But you can't. Concentrate on not falling. Fingers, hands, arms take the strain. Feet and legs swing away. Hang motionless. Silently stretching your spine. Start to pull up gently, steadily slowly.

Suddenly Tom shouts, 'Do you remember that time in the Dolomites?'

He does know. No Tom, not now.

'After we left you in the hospital, there didn't seem much point in staying on so we wandered back through the Tyrol. Sandra fell for an Italian chef. Said he had a villa on Capri or somewhere, so we separated. She never cared for climbing. Not like us. Can't understand why.'

Reach higher. Easier now – into the sunlight. Tom backlit, shadowed. Wearing a halo.

Feet back on the rock. Smile. The rest is easy. But oh, the pain in your back. Tom is ecstatic.

'Grand climb eh? What say we do another – Scorpion eh?'

'Let's save it for tomorrow. Rather have a couple of beers in the Old Dog.'

Surprisingly he agrees. I don't mention my back.

SNOWDON HORSESHOE

(Daylight Robbery)

By 1984, I was lecturing up and down the CEGB Northwest Region about asbestos identification and the measurement of airborne asbestos fibres. In December, I had an unexpected and welcome opportunity to complete a walk that I had longed to do for many years, albeit that on this occasion it would be in winter. I wrote the following essay sometime later. If I had merely written short notes about my ten best walks (my original intention a long time ago), this walk would have had first place. Today, it is still my favourite memory. I haven't mentioned this, but for safety, I left a note in the car with my expected time of return.

Suddenly I realised I wasn't alone. Below and to my right I sensed that a shadow was following me, moving at the same speed. I stopped to look round and saw, at an indeterminate distance, that several concentric rainbows had formed a halo round the shadow's head. The cause was simple enough. The Llanberis Valley had filled with cloud to form a pillow on which my shadow was resting. This day would become one of those for which the avid fell walker prays, a day to cheer up those miserable nights when raindrops spatter on the windows and hailstones crackle down the chimney.

'Carpe Diem' they say – 'Seize the Day'. So I had. There was not a cloud in the sky when my employers asked me at short notice on December 10th 1984, if I would travel to North Wales to do some business the next day. One look at the sky, followed by a little mental arithmetic, and I answered without hesitating, 'No problem. I'll set off immediately.'

I knew that with only two hours of driving I could be at the hostelry of Pen-y-Pass at the start of the Snowdon Horseshoe by mid-day. Four hours of daylight before darkness fell would be left for me to complete one of the most alluring ridge walks in the British Isles. The Horseshoe is not without danger and usually requires a full day for its completion. But I was fit from my years of fell-running and reckoned that I would have no trouble with the time. If I were wrong, I could easily drop off the ridge – not literally, you understand. I had no intention of becoming a mountain rescue statistic. I had calculated the risks finely and would travel light.

So there I was, approaching the knife edge ridge of Crib Goch where the walker can, honestly, sit astride the rocks with one leg dangling above the deep shadowed defile of Cwm Uchaf on the North side and the other over the gentler slopes to the South where a path serves the more fearful walker. Here I came upon a snag – even on such a sun blessed day the path was sheeted with ice, and I was wearing rubber soled trainers.

I had reached the ridge in under fifty minutes but now I was forced to inch my way gingerly along, using the crest as a handhold. I was conscious that the clock was ticking. However, beyond the pinnacles that terminate Crib Goch, the ridge widens and becomes runnable, and in well under two hours I was over half-way round and standing on Snowdon's summit.

I allowed myself to pause then to savour the experience. In every direction mountain peaks, suggestive of islands, were marooned in an ocean of cloud. Horizontal icicles decorated the summit cairn, the result of moisture laden freezing winds from the West. Two walkers clad in boots and wearing padded anoraks as if ready to climb Everest, emerged from the clouds carrying ice axes and toting heavy rucksacks on their backs. They looked askance at me in my shorts and trainers as if I were a nut case. We exchanged no more than a civil greeting as we passed, for I had no time to spare for small talk.

I left them on the summit no doubt enjoying the view as much as I had done and set off to complete the round by descending into the cloud. I was now so intent on finishing in daylight that in my arrogance, I omitted to check my compass and emerged below the clouds totally bemused to find a tremendous dry valley on my left where I had expected to see Llyn Llydaw. Obviously, I was not where I intended to be so, following some muttered expletives, I drew upon my memories of the mountain to carry out some mental gymnastics. A rapid assessment of the topography soon convinced

155

me that I was heading for Beddgelert. But you must understand – I was not lost. Being lost is more than not knowing where you are; there is the added factor of not knowing which way to go. I knew where I wanted to be and so had two options, either to contour the extra distance around the lower slopes of Snowdon's summit or drop into the depths of Cwm Tregalan which, unfortunately, would involve more climbing to regain the ridge.

Both courses would involve extra time. In the event I chose the latter course and was soon back on the path that leads over the summit of Y Lliwedd back to the car park. For the second time that day I climbed above the clouds, with just enough time to be aware of the sun setting far below me over the Lleyn Peninsula. From there, the descent was an easy run off down to the well-trodden Miners' Path, beloved by so many tourists. By 4.00pm I was back at my car and changing into a respectable business suit, while somewhere above the clouds, the stars began to shine as the evening shadows lengthened and December gloom descended on a silent world. Daylight robbery indeed.

Snowdon Horseshoe

EXILE IN INDIA

In 1987 I was offered a twelve-month secondment to provide chemical advice to the National Thermal Power Company of India, pertaining to the construction and operation of power stations. The major attraction was that I might be able to explore far more of the world than I had ever expected. Another attraction was that once I completed the twelve months, I could reclaim from the Inland Revenue all the income tax that been deducted from my salary while there. There were, however, two downsides: 1) I would be leaving my darling Brenda in England where she was employed as a Health Visitor, and 2) I would be away from my beloved British mountains.

Once the formal arrangements had been completed, I was due to fly out on September 1st, 1987. I knew I would be missing my mountains and would need a memory to sustain me so a few days before I left, I booked two nights for Brenda and myself at the Burnmoor Inn in Eskdale. From there, I was hoping, even if walking alone, to complete the Mosedale round from Wasdale Head – Yewbarrow, Red Pike, Pillar, Steeple, Kirk Fell and Great Gable. This, I guessed would be enough. Sadly, the weather didn't oblige, so the round would have to wait until I returned a year later. Instead, and after two very wet days, Brenda suggested, at 4.00 pm on the day we were due to return home, (also my penultimate day in England) that I should have a quick run up and down Great Gable. It was a generous gesture and one that I accepted gratefully despite the dark clouds that were still threatening overhead. In vest and shorts, on an indistinct track without a compass and navigating partly by wind direction, I reached the summit by way of Beckhead and was back down inside 90 minutes to join Brenda for an evening meal at the King George IV at Eskdale Green. Two days later I was on my way to India.

From a height of 20,000 ft on the glide path, I recognised the runway at Delhi airport quite easily by the international and domestic terminals at opposite ends. The planes around them resembled a litter of hungry piglets suckling from the teats of a recumbent sow. More interesting though, was a plume of smoke that started somewhere on the dusty horizon to cross the airport like a thin string of grey polluted wool. As we banked for our final descent, I could distinguish its source to be the twin smokestacks of what could only be a power station, interesting for me because the only reason for my arrival in India was to help the country, in its burgeoning need for electricity, to generate even more pollution.

The smell of India, about which I had been forewarned, was surprisingly absent on disembarking, though after a domestic flight later in the day, the stench of stale urine at Raipur provincial airport was so potent that I was forced to delay a comfort stop for several hours until my driver reached a stretch of road devoid of humanity. Until then, it had seemed as if the entire population of India had turned out to welcome me. After six hours of driving on execrable roads from Raipur, included in 30 hours of continuous travel, I reached Korba, my destination and the major town in that locality. My home for the next six months was in the newly constructed township of Jamni Pali that lay close by. There I could at last be alone.

Far from the tourist routes, I guessed that life was not going to be easy. On my first night, rats either ate or defecated on the favourite biscuits that I had imported from England, and by day three all the mosquitoes in the locality had discovered where I lived. The heat and humidity were overpowering for I had arrived towards the end of the monsoon and when the daily rains stopped, the ground dried out so rapidly that clouds of faecal infested dust soon re-filled the air. But the food there was tolerable, and I put up with the geckos that frequently scuttled across my bedroom ceiling – they were supposed to keep the mosquitoes under control.

Public holidays of every faith were observed, and since there were Christians, Hindus and Muslims working on site, each faith with its own festivals, work ceased for a holy day far more frequently than in England. Furthermore, Health and Safety regulations appeared to be non-existent, and work stopped for a day every time there was a fatality, of which there were far too many. Construction, therefore, proceeded exceedingly slowly, and

158

because the bureaucracy was incredibly involved, spare parts for instruments and machinery were only obtainable after interminable delays. Consequently, because I was too far from a telephone, I had too little to do and too much time in which to do it.

In theory, the economy was dependent on providing employment for all, so wherever I looked, I saw women carrying stones, cement, sand or rocks. In effect, the same labour force that built the pyramids was still operating. When I queried why no heavy machinery was used on site, I received a reply that I ought to have known in advance – one machine would put 200 women out of work, followed by inevitable starvation. Living in the comparative comfort of my own concrete apartment, the shanty town outside the station gates where these same women lived in squalor changed my views on poverty forever. Four-foot diameter drainpipes waiting to be installed were homes for the lucky ones. The educated Indian attitude to work, moreover, was another matter. One example will suffice. Two months after my arrival, the senior manager of the National Thermal Power Company of India called to discuss progress. I was away from the office when he arrived. On my return I heard him listening on his portable radio to an Indian/Australian Test Match while chewing his stock of betel nuts – no doubt needed to steady his nerves, because India lost by one run. All that day he would brook no interruption!

At such times I wondered what I was doing there. I went with the honourable intention of assisting a (so-called) backward, or at least a developing, nation to haul itself into the world of modern technology. Instead, I experienced much that was redolent of past ages juxtaposed against an industry that would, I supposed, inevitably play a major part in contributing to global warming. Truly, the atmospheric emissions that I saw on my arrival caused me to wonder if I should have stayed in England. Whatever the case, one thing I now know for certain is that whether or not I helped to change India, India certainly changed me.

During the journey by road from Raipur to Korba, I had been hoping for a view of something that might be worth a small exploration, but I had arrived in the late afternoon and night had fallen well before my driver reached Jamni Pali and the company guest house where I was to be housed until I had an apartment of my own. Of course, I was seriously jet-lagged and never heard the heavy rain that fell during the night. I was awakened at 11.30am the next morning by an Indian in a white and smartly belted uniform of what I supposed was that of a waiter, because he told me that although breakfast had finished long ago, I might still have a simple meal of toast and a boiled egg. After breakfast, I went outside to explore the immediate area where the rains of the night had filled the ruts left by countless bullock carts, bicycles and rickshaws between patches of sun-dried mud that steamed in the heat of an oppressive afternoon.

Despite the overnight rain that should have cleared the air, there were no distant views to be had through the now heavily dust-laden haze, so there was little point in spending too much time in speculation. Eventually, I would have my own apartment from the flat roof of which I could see, in the distance, a hill that seemed to stand alone from its neighbours. It was clearly too far to reach on foot and I guessed it was on the far side of the Hasdeo River that supplied cooling water to the power station. I decided I would need a bicycle and at the first opportunity, I would ride out and investigate.

I had to wait three months until a bicycle became available, and even then it came with a twisted inner tube in the rear tyre. It came as no surprise to find that that the inner tube was also punctured and had multiple patches on previous repairs. Nor did it come with a puncture repair kit. Such is one example of the problems of life in what was then effectively, at worst an open prison and at best, a holiday complex without the usual amenities.

By mid-January I had the bike suitably fixed up and when an opportunity to explore presented itself, I took it. Despite the January night-time temperature falling to near zero, it rose rapidly once the sun was up and by mid-day could be in the mid-eighties. I prepared as well as I could by ensuring that I had two litres of filtered and boiled water to carry with me, but of course in such an

160

area I could find no map of any kind. Some of the local Indians told me there were supposed to be defensive fortifications on top – perhaps a hill fort of some antiquity.

I set off at sunrise – about 7.00am, hoping to have completed my explorations in good time before the heat of the day became too much. I'd been told that a path left the main road to the city of Raipur at Chhuri, a village that I remembered passing through when making frequent visits to Bilaspur, the local administrative centre. By 7.30, I'd made good progress and turned off the road as directed in search of Chhuri village centre. I experienced no more than a few inquisitive glances from the women working in the fields on either side. I came across several wooden grids on the ground that resembled palettes. These aroused my curiosity until I realised they were used to make the mud bricks from which the village houses were built.

The exit from Chhuri was more difficult to find than the entrance – a number of paths led away, but the one I chose seemed more used than the others because it was heavily rutted (shades of Robert Frost and his poem –*The Road Not Taken*). I was soon alone but for one bullock cart that passed me going in the opposite direction. The driver gave me a quizzical look as he passed, as if he thought I were weak in the head. At least I was on some kind of track wherever it led, but the rutted nature of the ground made it impossible to ride, as anyone will know who's had the misfortune to have a front wheel stuck in old fashioned tram lines.

After a couple of hours of pushing, I reached the top of a rocky escarpment that showed signs of wear from the metal clad wheels of countless carts, and I could see the river far below. But I was disappointed to see the hill beyond it. By now the day had warmed up considerably and having walked and pushed my bicycle most of the way from Chhuri, I took a long drink from my water reserves. The slope to the river was too steep to ride down so I had to resort to proceeding again on foot. At the river I sat down despondently, for the river at that point was about 100 metres wide. I could only guess at what hazards waited for me below the surface – and how deep was it anyway?

As I gazed at the hill across the river and ruminated on my misfortune, a second bullock cart appeared on the far bank and began to cross. At no point did the water reach higher than the axles! Once the cart was on its way up the escarpment behind me, I changed into my flip-flops and waded across, still pushing the bicycle. But there was a stretch of dry sand on the far side through which, again, it was impossible to ride. Once more I was reduced to more physical labour and was again very much in need of another drink.

The unclimbed hill by the Hasdeo River
January 24th, 1987

Suitably refreshed, but with diminishing reserves of water, I pushed on using whatever stretches of dry rideable ground I could find, but I soon reached a forest of impassable tangled undergrowth. I was greatly disappointed to have come so far and be probably less than a mile from my objective, only to be thwarted by a natural obstacle. But I needed water for my return journey and the sun was so high that it was telling me what I already knew. It was time to call it a day.

Even if I'd taken a machete and conquered the undergrowth, I doubt if I could have climbed alone what appeared to be sheer cliffs above the tree line. I returned safely but with little water left. A bottle of Indian beer (Golden Eagle) straight from the fridge had the restorative power of nectar. Soon after that, I transferred to a second power station where I spent my final six months, so I never had a chance to return to that enticing hill. On the other hand, I had somewhere else to explore.

The rail journey to my second posting at Ramagundam (translates as The Furnace of Rama) in Andra Pradesh about 50 miles north of Hyderabad, again involved a stretch of overnight travel and I arrived in the early morning without any means of transport to the power station about five miles away. There ought to have been a taxi waiting for me, but not for the first time, Indian communications had broken down somewhere and I had to fend for myself.

I hired a three-wheeled, black and yellow painted *tuk tuk,* also known disparagingly as a "cockroach". My arrival at the Company guest house by this means caused a little consternation amongst the senior staff, lest I should report to higher authority such lack of the proper respect due to a visiting specialist. At least the journey from the rail station had given me a view of an interesting rocky peak quite close to the plant where I was to spend my final working days in India.

The town of Ramagundam is well named for the daytime temperature frequently reaches 45 degrees Celsius during the summer – much too hot to climb the only little hill in the area. However, once the monsoon arrived, the temperature dropped remarkably, although the humidity simultaneously approached 100% and clouds obscured the sun. Heavy rain fell, seemingly mostly at night, and filled every depression on the road to work, sometimes to a depth that would force me to return home until the afternoon when the floods had usually receded.

It was late July, on a cool day that was also a public holiday before I had a chance to climb the peak. I cycled to the nearest point on the road and set off through a shanty town of scarcely waterproof, thatched mud huts between which a fast-flowing and ill-smelling stream barred my path. I cast up and down the stream before I found a row of stepping-stones in front of a small mud walled chapel with a sign over the door – BETHEL. I was told later that it was considered essential to cross water before worshipping, but I can't vouch for the truth of that.

Ramagundam Power Station
(about two miles away)
July 25th, 1988

I soon left the dwellings behind for an uphill trudge through a waste of pathless scrub and broken rocks, always on the lookout for snakes even though I knew that any snakes would sense my coming and slither away in fear. After about an hour I was at the summit, such as it was – a pile of rocks with a "window" through which I took a photo of the power station – more to prove that I'd been there than for posterity.

I decided against climbing ten feet higher up vertical rocks to the very top, fearing that nobody would be around to help should I fall. I varied my descent route and came upon a quarry where a dozen or so women were breaking large rocks into smaller ones, probably to be used as hard core for road construction. An Indian gentleman smoking a cigarette was lounging nearby alongside a lorry and trailer. He clearly had no intention of helping them, so I supposed him to be the lorry driver waiting for his next load.

Another month would see me home again in England after a year during which I'd climbed one small hill and failed to climb another. My life amongst the hills of Britain would soon be back to normal.

A BOX OF DELIGHTS

1. In June 1968, we took our girls to the Isle of Arran for a week of exploration. The girls were both involved with Brownie Guiding projects. Kathryn was identifying wild flowers and Rosalind was collecting various types of seashells. When on holiday as a family we had a democratic system whereby each of us would choose an activity for one day, in which the others would take part. Naturally, my choice would be a big expedition – on this holiday it would be the ascent of Goat Fell (2866 ft).

The boring nature of the ascent by the "tourist" route from Brodick, which Brenda and Kathryn decided to forego, having climbed to about 2,400 ft, was more than offset by the astounding view of sheer naked rock that Rosalind and I beheld on gaining the summit. The absence of verticality was of no significance. It was amazing that so much shattered rock could be compressed into so small a space that not even a single blade of grass relieved the ground beneath our feet. Rock, and nothing but rock, was lord and master there. Rock dominated – the rock on which we stood was rough, tough and unyielding, and it seemed that even the many names carved upon it would soon be gone, leaving primaeval barrenness to reign supreme.

This, if anywhere, was the birthplace of the Isle of Arran. It seemed as if the rocks had a life of their own and had used their naked strength to force their way through the skin of the world, pushing aside the delicate fields and wooded glens below. In the Lake District, the transition from the pastoral tranquillity of Borrowdale to the shattered rocks of Scafell is gradual. Here the change was immediate and dramatic. On the day we left the island, not a single cloud disturbed the crystal blue of the morning sky. The MV Glen Sannox steamed into Brodick Bay and I photographed her with Goatfell etched clear against the sky, a picture of peace and serenity never to be forgotten. It was difficult to believe that behind that scene lay a land of unforgiving brutal stone.

2. In June 1971, with both girls on holiday with school, Brenda and I booked into the Borrowdale Hotel. Apart from climbing Glaramara, as reported later [page 227], we had a good day out climbing Haystacks from Gatescarth Farm and followed that with Fleetwith Pike. At Dubs quarry I was delighted to come upon an Elastoplast tin which I duly opened. I wasn't surprised to find, as I expected, that it was a check point for, I guessed, an OBMS expedition. With a certain amount of hubris, I added my name (which would be a surprise for whoever collected it) and an explanation. While we were there, the sun broke through the previously unbroken cloud and gave us some dramatic views of Great Gable. We descended from Fleetwith Pike directly to Gatescarth, as straight as the flight of an arrow, although Brenda wasn't too happy with the exposure, safe though it was. She only felt comfortable and able to relax once the road was beneath her feet.

On Fleetwith Pike looking to Great Gable
June 1971

167

3. Both Brenda and I had, and I still have, an interest in history, so that in 1981 when both the girls were off on their own holidays, we went to Crete in May. As any historian will know, the main historical attractions on the island are the ruins of the palace of Knossos. That was not the only reason for choosing Crete, though. For a walker there are a number of spectacular gorges, the most famous being the Gorge of Samaria. The walk begins on the Plain of Omalos at 1,250 metres above sea level and ends on the shore of the Libyan Sea at the village of Agia Roumeli, so I knew that it would be downhill all the way and that Brenda would have no trouble completing it. We had chosen to stay in Malia, not realising that we would be almost as far away from the gorge as it is possible to be on Crete. To get to the start we were picked up at 5.30am by a coach that stopped at so many places on the way that it was 10.00am by the time we arrived at the Plain of Omalos. By then we were both so hungry that a plate of honey and Greek yoghurt was exactly the stimulation we needed to help us continue.

The early stages of the descent are nicely tree shaded, so it was pleasantly cool in the shade at that time of day. Lower down we passed the village of Samaria that gives the gorge its name but was abandoned in 1962 when the gorge became a National Park. From that point, the trees gradually became fewer, and the heat increased until, as we approached the most spectacular part of the gorge known as "The Iron Gates", where the vertical cliff walls are a mere four metres apart and rise to a height of almost 300 metres, there was no shade at all. There, the afternoon heat became intense. Beyond the "iron gates" the sea was still two kilometres away, but an enterprising woman was selling soft drinks from the gate of her cottage. Whatever the price, those drinks were worth every drachma. Because there's no road to the village, we had to wait for a ferry to take us back to our coach. On board there was a stampede to the bar for drinks. I was very annoyed when a large man pushed in before me and, although the barman had seen me and knew I was waiting, he served the intruder. Then he turned to me, but before I could say anything, he put his finger to his nose and whispered, 'He German – I charge him double.' Clearly the war had not been forgotten.

4. On Saturday March 3rd, 1984, Brenda attended a Health Visitors' Conference in London so I took the opportunity for a Lakeland walk over snow covered hills. I intended this to be a solo walk and, knowing that the night-time temperatures had been below freezing for some days, I took my ice axe. Rosalind accompanied me to Coniston where we separated. She took our little dog, Sam, for a gentle stroll, probably through Tilberthwaite, while I was on the fells.

My plan was to follow the Coniston fell race route beginning up Mouldry Bank and then follow it as far as the top of Wetherlam, which by then I knew well. From there I would continue to follow the race route as far as Swirl How from where I would drop down to the Three Shire Stone and then climb Pike 'o Blisco and Lingmoor before meeting Rosalind back in Coniston. It was a glorious day with not a single cloud in the sky and the semi-frozen snow on the lower slopes crunched delightfully beneath my trainers.

The higher I climbed the more ice and snow I encountered, especially where the sun had only penetrated briefly. It was as well that I had taken my ice axe for my rubber soled trainers were useless wherever I could find no exposed rocks or grassy tussocks to gain a purchase. From Wetherlam I headed towards Swirl How to find that Prison Band had almost taken on the appearance of an Alpine snow-covered ridge.

I managed to navigate over the frozen slopes of Swirl How itself using the ice axe for balance as a third leg, and soon passed the Three Shire Stone on my way to Pike o' Blisco and Lingmoor. From there, it was an easy walk down to the road and a return to Coniston. All day, the distant views of the snow-covered Helvellyn range and the central fells were something to die for.

Prison Band on Swirl How pretending to be Alpine
March 3rd 1984

5. Brenda and I spent August Bank holiday 1984 staying in Ravenglass. The rest of the Lake District was seemingly booked up, so we were able to enjoy a quiet gentle stroll over Muncaster Fell and catch La'al Ratty on the way back from Eskdale Green.

Ross's Camp on Muncaster Fell
August 1984

We'd done the same walk in 1975, also on a Bank holiday, while staying at the Woolpack Inn in Eskdale. On that occasion, we'd left the car at Boot and taken the train to Ravenglass and had seen no one all day. It was a walk that Brenda had managed easily, but this time we would take our time to savour the solitude and feel sorry for the crowds that would be infesting the more popular Lakeland fells. We stopped for lunch at Ross's Camp long enough for me to sketch my own version of stones that might be taken to be a megalithic chambered tomb. However, Mr Wainwright explains that it was erected by a Victorian shooting party, possibly from Muncaster Castle, to be used as a dining table.

171

During our second visit, again, there was nobody else on the fell, so the first people we spoke to were at Eskdale Green station where we caught the baby train back to Ravenglass. We slept that night to the sound of whimbrels calling over the sandbanks that guard the confluence of the three rivers Irt, Mite and Esk.

6. In May 1986, we went to Skye but had a week of terrible weather that precluded climbing anything of note. But on one day I managed a run through Glen Sligachan. We had stayed many years before at "Ashbank", a farmhouse on the road to Elgol. The farmhouse featured then on a picture-postcard, together with an alluring view of Blaven that formed a majestic backdrop.

This time it was good to drive past and recall the days when our girls had played by Loch Slapin while sheep grazed on the pebble-strewn shore. The distance from Elgol to Sligachan is about eleven miles so it would be an easy run. The height gained is very little, although the scenery is tremendous. The first few miles follow the shore of Loch Scavaig with unforgettable views of the main Cuillin Ridge always in sight. The path never rises enough to give a good view into the fastness of Loch Coruisk but I knew it was there, connected to Loch Scavaig by, some say, the shortest river in Scotland.

I tried to pick out the Inaccessible Pinnacle on top of Sgurr Dearg, but I couldn't make it out. Every step of the way I had to watch where I was putting my feet and I encountered more wider and deeper streams than I'd expected. This wasn't too much of a worry though, because I was wearing my fell-running shoes. The route is basically a straight line South to North so there was no danger of getting lost, and about six miles into the run the Sligachan Hotel comes into sight. There then follows the curious phenomenon that a distant object never seems to get any closer, no matter how long you continue to run, until suddenly you look up and realise that you are less than a mile away. There must surely be an mathematical exponential formula to explain this. And then, when you arrive, there on the hotel car park is your faithful Brenda waiting with the car.

7. When I returned from India in 1988, I was suffering from severe headaches and was diagnosed as having an enlarged liver, possibly due to an amoebic infection, twelve months of daily anti-malarial medication, or excessive drinking. Take your pick. Anyway, I went "on the wagon" for three months and by April 1989 when I finished last in the Coniston fell race, I had recovered much of the fitness that I had lost from a year without any chance of any training runs. In that race, I knew I wasn't fully recovered, so ran most of the way in company with Jimmy Niblett, an elderly veteran member of Horwich RMI who kept complaining about one of his knees. In deference to his age, I let him finish in front of me – next to last. I would run the race twice more, on each occasion with steadily improving times.

8. In July 1989, I forgot what I'd learned about taking a direct line to a summit and set off to climb straight to the top of Red Pike, having left Brenda at the Fish Hotel in Buttermere. I soon met heather that, being on such a steep slope, was level with my face. There was no way I could progress through anything like that, so I had to divert to the accepted path. Once on the ridge though, I had a splendid run/walk over High Stile, High Crag, Haystacks and Fleetwith Pike, and was back at the Fish Hotel in three and a half hours. A week later Brenda attended a Health Visitors' Conference, so with Kathryn I completed the middle section of the Bob Graham circuit from Dunmail Raise to Wasdale, her husband Peter acting as our chauffeur. It was such a bad day that we set off wearing full waterproofs in heavy rain that persisted all the way to Rossett Pike. The swirling clouds and a Westerly gale that had sprung up made for slow progress owing to the need for accurate navigation. It was about there that I thought about abandoning the run but a slight improvement in the weather and a discussion with Kathryn changed my mind and we completed the section in six hours and fifty minutes.

***Start of the second leg of the Bob Graham round
with Kathryn, at Dunmail Raise
July 29ᵗʰ 1989***

9. For a short break in late August 1989, I booked three nights for Brenda and myself at the Burnmoor Inn in Boot. At last I had a chance to run the Mosedale Horseshoe which had been my goal before I left for India two years earlier. The weather was superb with cloud shadows dappling the fields and fellsides. Sadly, Brenda had a slight tummy upset but was happy to sit by Wastwater and rest, have a drink and a snack at the Wastwater Hotel and chat to a National Trust warden. Meanwhile I had a good jog/walk over Yewbarrow and Red Pike where Joss Naylor passed me running down as I climbed up. This time I didn't sit in "The Chair" but continued straight on to Scoat Fell and Steeple where, by perching my camera on a rock and setting the delayed action, I took what is today called a "selfie". From there I continued my run over Pillar to the top of Black Sail Pass, followed by Kirk Fell and Great

Gable, the actual summit of which, owing to the crowds, I avoided and raced down to Wasdale via Beckhead to meet Brenda less than four and a half hours after leaving her – it had been a circuit worth waiting for two years to complete.

10. In July 1995, Rosalind accompanied us to stay for a week on Skye. We took the ferry from Glenelg which gave us a chance, on the way, to visit the location of Camusfearna, the name that Gavin Maxwell gave to his cottage where he wrote *Ring of Bright Water*. Owing to bad weather, I have never yet had a chance to climb any of the peaks on the main Cuillin Ridge, and I know now that, owing to my age and infirmities, I never will. However, during that week on Skye, we took the car across to Raasay where Brenda explored by car and Rosalind and I walked to Hallaig and climbed, Dun Caan, the only hill on the island, by a "sporting" (i.e. pathless) route, hoping for the best. The hill resembles an inverted funnel with a very steep finish above what felt like a 45° slope. It was a very satisfying climb, but rain prevented us from lingering, so we returned by sundry paths without an exact knowledge of where we were heading. But my instinct proved correct, as it so often has, and we found Brenda and the car at some ruined mine buildings, both of us looking like drowned rats.

On another wet day, with Rosalind, I climbed the imposing Blaven that I had admired since my first view of the mountain in 1964 when we'd stayed at "Ashbank", the farmhouse referred to in 6. above. In 1964, in true Outward Bound style, every day I had braved the waters of Loch Slapin for a dip before breakfast. But now I was aged fifty eight and thought that Blaven was a better option. On this occasion, despite having tried to understand the guide-book directions, I set off with Rosalind on the wrong side of a stream. I soon realised my mistake, so we crossed over the stream and by various routes climbed into swirling clouds with me keeping the guide-book to hand. Even so we still managed to find ourselves somewhere that bore no resemblance to the guide-book, so that I frequently had to climb ahead and reconnoitre. We had climbed into an area where the rocks and scree were extremely loose and unstable. On one such advance I dislodged a boulder that went bounding down the scree to come to rest who knows where. It must have weighed several hundredweight and I shouted a warning although I knew that I was well to the side of Rosalind who would be in no danger. But suddenly the mist cleared, and we could see the Blaven ridge close above us. We descended from the summit by the south ridge with tremendous views in all directions to meet Brenda on the road where there were many more cars parked than when we'd begun our climb.

Blaven
July 1995

11. In 1995, Kathryn and her husband, Peter, emigrated to New Zealand. On November 11[th,] two weeks before Peter departed (Kathryn would follow him later), I took her round the Kentmere Horseshoe fell-race route on a day of mist and rain. Visibility was not good, but I had no doubt about my navigational skills and they served me well as we ran, jogged or walked, I in my best relaxed fell-running style. Kathryn had already proved her abilities, being a member of the Keswick Ladies Team in 1993, a year when the team won the English Fell Running Championship. Where once I had been the faster, now our positions were reversed, although I reckoned I was still the better navigator. At the top of the Nan Bield Pass we encountered a group of four lads and stopped for a chat. They were lost and seemed confused, not only as to where they were, but also as to where they had left their car. All I could do was show them where they were on their map, hoping that they could work it out for themselves. It would be a long walk back over the pass if they dropped into the wrong valley. It was the last outing on the Lakeland fells for Kathryn before she left three months later to join Peter.

12. A year later (January 1997), Brenda and I went for a long holiday in New Zealand, driving a hired car through North and South Islands. Eventually we joined Kathryn and Peter and stayed for a couple of weeks where they had settled in Arrowtown. Unlike the "freedom to roam" that we enjoy in Britain, much of New Zealand is either forested, private, sacred to the Maori or impassable. But the hiking trails are well cared for and a delight to run or walk on. We were close to Arrowtown before I had a chance to try a short run on one of the trails, many of which take several days to complete. The Kepler track begins at the lake Te Anau "Control Gates" – not to limit access to the track but to control the level of the lake. Brenda dropped me off there on a fine sunny day, and I set off hoping to reach the Luxmore Hut – the mid-point of the trail where those wishing to complete the trail spend a night. The estimated time to the hut for a walker was given as 8-10 hours, but I had run through the Lairig Ghru four years before and still thought I could make it to the hut and back in much less time than that.

I started easily with a gentle jog/walk along the lake shore for forty minutes on a path of beech mast that was dry and well maintained. Several bridges, floored with chicken wire, helped with crossing the boggy stretches. As soon as the track turned off, I began to climb for a further hour and ten minutes through interminable bush and passed through a spectacular band of

177

limestone cliffs, complete with wooden ladders and walkways. Eventually I estimated that I emerged from the bush at a height of about 1,000 metres into a gale force wind, together with rain (for which I donned my waterproofs). This was sweeping over typical Lake District high country through which the narrow path threaded its way between tussocky grasses to reach the hut at a height of 1,085 metres. I ate my lunch inside the hut along with other visitors, most of whom I guessed would be staying the night. On the descent, before reaching the bush, I made a 10 minute detour to the Luxmore Cave, just as the sun came out and the rain stopped. But I didn't have a torch with me, so I didn't venture more than a few feet inside what I expect is a cavers' paradise. My overall time to the hut and back to Te Anau was less than five hours. It was yet another splendid solo day, despite not climbing to a summit.

13. Two years later we went to New Zealand again, giving me an opportunity to fulfil a lifetime's ambition to visit the grave of Robert Louis Stevenson (RLS) on top of Mount Vaea on the island of Upolu in Western Samoa. For our first visit to New Zealand, we had travelled east and stayed for three days in Singapore. This time we would travel west to visit Hawaii, followed by my choice of Samoa. Our Hawaii hotel was in Waikiki, close enough to allow us to walk to, and explore an extinct volcano, Diamond Head, which is well known for its wartime historical associations. It also includes a hiking trail. It's a little over 600 ft high and is a National State Monument covering an area of 475 acres, including a saucer-shaped crater. The trail to the highest point involves passing through a tunnel on a concrete walkway into the crater, from where the ascent continues up steep stairs through a lamp-lit 225-ft long tunnel. At the start of the steepest section, I left Brenda behind to explore the crater and went on to the summit for a fine view over Waikiki. It's an interesting place for industrial archaeologists and geologists as well as walkers. The tourist board recommend that you wear good shoes, carry water and wear a sun hat and sunscreen. It also tells you that the last tenth of a mile is all stairs and is especially steep and you should allow 1.5 to 2 hours. I was back with Brenda within 30 minutes of leaving her even though I had to wait to ascend the stairs, owing to others descending through the narrow tunnel. An interesting experience but not as satisfying as my climb to the grave of my hero.

Born in 1850, Robert Louis Stevenson endured a lifetime of pulmonary problems. Possibly hoping that the warmth and humidity of the South Pacific Island of Western Samoa would assist his breathing, he emigrated and built a house there that he named Vailima. The house stands at the foot of the 1,400 ft Mount Vaea, to the top of which in 1894, his body was carried for burial by the island's chiefs, so much was he loved by them.

Our hotel was too far from Vailima for me to have an early morning run, however cool it might be, so we hired a taxi for the morning. There is a charge of 15 Western Samoan dollars to enter the Vailima estate, but for me it was worth every cent. The entrance to the house is filled with Stevenson memorabilia – books by him, books about him, and photos galore of him, his family and Samoan women. We had our guide to ourselves which was lucky because he told us that the day before, six coach loads of tourists from a cruise ship had arrived, as well as others like ourselves arriving by taxi. There was a serene calm over the whole estate, so we were able to appreciate the varied aspects of the RLS menage as we visited room after room, each one mirroring its occupant's character – RLS himself, Fanny (his wife), his mother, and Isobel (step-daughter) and Austin (step-grandson).

For me, being familiar from reading about his family, it was a magical experience. We left the guide at the house. Then, while Brenda sat by a shaded stream close to a bridge that we discovered, made from two halves of a split tree trunk, I set off to climb to his grave. The path was delightfully shaded for most of the way, and easy enough to follow if I kept moving steeply upwards. I was sorely tempted at times to take what looked like easier side paths but feared that if I did so I might be unable to find my way back through apparently impenetrable jungle. The path was frequently wet and slippery but eventually the angle of ascent eased, and I arrived at a small clearing where a shallow concrete plinth supported a white painted structure resembling a house. Despite a notice asking visitors to desist, his grave was sadly disfigured with graffiti.

Robert Louis Stevenson's final resting place
on top of Mount Vaea. The Pacific ocean is just visible.
February 3ʳᵈ 1999

RLS's own epitaph, cast in bronze is attached to the side:

Under the wide and starry sky,
Dig the grave and let me lie
Glad did I live and gladly die,
And I laid me down with a will.

This be the verse you grave for me
Here he lies where he longed to be
Home is the sailor, home from the sea
And the hunter home from the hill.

Fanny was buried beside him in 1914, which I didn't know. The view to Apia below was quite beautiful and the only sound was that of birdsong and a gentle whispering of the wind in the tree-tops. I wondered why I was brought to the brink of tears as I thought of RLS, buried so far from the land of his birth yet lying there where he longed to be. Forty five minutes after leaving Brenda I was back with her.

The ascent had been hot and the humidity probably 100% so my silk shirt, bought in Hawaii, was saturated with sweat and I drank freely from the water bottle that I'd left with Brenda.

Note: I may have been fortunate that in 1999, the top of Mount Vaea was accessible. When Kathryn, and Peter, on holiday from New Zealand some years later, visited Vailima, access to the top was closed owing to the great number of trees that had fallen across the path during a violent storm.

From the notes that I made, I wrote this poem much later:

Homage To R.L.S

Far from the loch and the salty spray
Vailima stands red-roofed and grey,
home of the writer who wished he could be
home from the mountain and home from the sea.

His spirit still lingers in silent rooms
where the breezes smell of hibiscus blooms.
His velvet jacket hangs loose on the door
by the leather boots that he always wore.

The couch where he lay is empty now
and coughing no longer furrows his brow.
Both paper and pen are laid aside
and the inkwell's fluid has long since dried.

Many are those who come with a will
to visit his home at the foot of the hill,
but few climb to see where he lodges in peace
in his windowless house with its infinite lease,

for steep is the path to the grove where he rests
where the buzzard, the eagle and hawk build their nests.
No sound but the whisper of wind in the trees
looking over the forest to tropical seas.

Not here are the burns that his feet loved to cross,
not Highland the rocks, the stones and the moss.
But the sun and the moon and the stars that caress
are the same shining over my rare R.L.S.

FOOT AND MOUTH

2001 was a bad year for all outdoor pursuits. Access to the Lake District fells was severely restricted by an outbreak of foot and mouth disease causing most outdoor enthusiasts to find their own responses to the epidemic. At Easter we parked the car at Windermere, crossed the lake on the ferry and spent a day on the roads, walking from Ferry House. At least the fells were in sight if not beneath my feet. I could see but couldn't touch.

But the Isle of Arran was one place that wasn't out of bounds and somewhere I could go to climb, so Brenda and I booked a week in a B & B in Lamlash overlooking Holy Island. We had mixed weather and refreshed our memories of when we'd stayed in Whiting Bay with the children thirty-three years earlier. We had several low-level walks which Brenda relished and one day, she dropped me off at Corrie from where I climbed Goatfell's northern ridge by way of Glen Sannox, wearing my usual lightweight running gear. It was cold and windy on the ridge but, once I was over the summit and descending to Brodick, I could enjoy the sunshine. I ran down the long descent quite easily, noticing many (possibly imagined) admiring glances of several walkers on their way to the top.

This would be our major holiday that year, so we continued by taking the ferry from Lochranza to the Mull of Kintyre to drive north to Oban for another week. This was another chance to indulge in a spot of nostalgia and recall the events of thirty-eight years earlier. That holiday, in May 1963, was our first holiday in Scotland. We'd driven our three-wheeled, soft-top Reliant Regal to stay at Benderloch, about eight miles north of Oban. At that time, the Connell Ferry Railway Bridge that lies above the Falls of Lora between Benderloch and Oban was shared between the railway and the road. Expecting that we would make good use of the bridge, I bought a pass for the week. It would prove to be a wise decision because, although the weather that May was excellent, Brenda had a severe asthma attack soon after we arrived. She was so bad that she was transferred to the Argyll Chest Hospital in Oban where she spent the week, leaving me to care for Rosalind and Kathryn, then aged three and two respectively.

Breathless in Oban

Without any warning suddenly
you couldn't speak. Breathless.
The attack was not announced,
so the crisis grew rapidly.
Impotent, I watched
you leaning,
heaving, your
forearms furrowing
deep on the biting ridge
of the iron frame at the open
window, gasping for air
like a landed, stranded fish.

Later, with the children safely
put to bed, I raced
each evening visiting
as a madness of seagulls
screamed after a tractor
burrowing deep into a field
Until the day when they
let you walk from the ward
to McCaig's Folly, where you
filled your lungs with the Hebrides
and the sunset took my breath away.

Now thirty-eight years later, I remembered leaving the girls each night in the guest house in the care of the other guests (who also had young children and so were sympathetic). I also recalled the hasty drive across the bridge each night and the road up to the hospital above the town. It stood about a couple of hundred yards away from McCaig's

Folly, so we thought we'd try to find it again. The road seemed vaguely familiar but now it was almost completely overgrown and so narrow that I began to wonder if it might be private. Fortunately, we met nothing coming down and the old parking space at the top was deserted. All that remained were the foundations of the isolation block and the two hospital Pavilions. Apart from the dereliction, everything was as I remembered. Nobody was about as we walked to McCaig's Folly and I wrote the above poem.

Before we left Oban in 2001, I climbed Ben Cruachan. Brenda meanwhile had a tour of the Loch Awe pumped storage hydro-electricity power station and a sail on Loch Etive. She parked at the power station visitor centre from where I set off wondering how I could get across the railway line that connects Oban to the rest of the world. I soon found the railway underpass that allows access to the mountain – it's on the Dalmally side of the visitor centre. The walk through a small wood of oak, birch and hazel was pleasant and wind free before I climbed steeply and steadily to the dam. I couldn't see the dam at that stage, but it soon came in sight as the path continued upwards. Once I reached the dam, I could see a metal ladder that I climbed to cross to the left side of the dam along which I continued to a cart track on the far side.

The summit was now obscured by mist that had developed while I'd been climbing, but I'd seen enough to know that the route veered to the right and I had my compass to hand. Added to that, it began to rain, and I was gradually becoming colder and wetter. I was on the point of giving in when the rain stopped and the mist opened up the view ahead to reveal the ridge. The prospect continued to be less than appealing when the ridge disappeared into cloud again, but the wind had dropped and I was becoming warmer, probably due to my extra exertion on the steeper slope.

Once in the mist I only needed to follow the path, even though in places it was indistinct. A man, and a boy whom I supposed to be his son, passed me on their way down and confirmed that I was on the right track. I continued upwards to come across a waste of scree and shattered rock and eventually a stubby "trig-point" amidst a ring of huge boulders that I took to be the summit. Beyond it the ground fell away so steeply that I guessed it would be the northern face. Somewhere out there to the north I thought, Brenda would be enjoying her sail, possibly in sunshine, while here was I with nothing to see except a circle of grey rain-soaked rock.

I set off down the track that I'd ascended and at the same time made a note of the compass bearing. But the constant need to watch where I was putting my feet must have caused me to deviate so far, that when I emerged from the mist I wasn't where I expected to be. A careful scrutiny of the view told me I was too far West, so I contoured East and after a few hundred yards came to the proper path. It was only a small deviation, but an example of the need for careful navigation when travelling in unknown country. I was never in any danger, and despite the rain and wind and a lack of views from the summit, it had been a satisfying day to ascend the highest Munro in Argyll.

By July 2001, although the lower pastures and intake fields were still subject to foot and mouth regulations, public access to the central fells of the Lake District was permitted. Buckets of disinfectant were still in place at each access point though, and in many places, notices informed walkers that a particular footpath was still closed. We were staying at the Burnmoor Inn at Boot in Eskdale and we'd taken Rosalind's dog, Sally, with us. As usual we did several low-level walks, mostly on roads and permitted tracks.

One day I managed to fit in both of the Scafells, starting of course from Boot. The O.S. map shows stone circles on Burnmoor that I'd never seen, so I made a detour to investigate before I reached Burnmoor Tarn. Walking across the moor I came across a sheep's skull long ago picked clean by crows. It would be a nice souvenir of the walk so I took it with me. From Burnmoor Tarn I made an easy ascent of Scafell by Hardrigg Gill, encountering a solitary walker on the way. From the summit I dropped down to Fox's Tarn because I intended to return from Scafell Pike by way of Lords Rake. Once on the Pike side of Cam Spout I could rest and have my lunch while watching the climbers on Scafell's East Buttress.

I was soon over the Pike and at the bottom of Lord's Rake. There I was surprised to find much less scree than I'd been accustomed to. I thought to myself then, that mountains are not as eternally unchangeable as most people think. Not only that, but half-way up, I came across a massive boulder that bridged the Rake from left to right – another example of mountain mutability. It was difficult, but not impossible, to climb over it. I read much later in a *Cumbria* magazine that Lord's Rake had been declared a dangerous place to visit. At the top of the Rake I reached the back side of a notice which, when I turned back to look at it, informed me "This footpath is closed to walkers". Whether it was because of foot and mouth or the recently fallen boulder I have no idea. On the way back to Boot, I caught up with the solitary walker that I'd met earlier and he told me that he'd contented himself with climbing Scafell. It was a day when I'd collected a number of unexpected trifles, mostly memories, but also the sheep's skull about which I wrote the following poem.

Charcoal

He releases power locked inside a clutch
of charcoal sticks and with perspective
mutilates snow whiteness.
With depths of greys and blacks
he dimples oranges,
draws hollows fit for apple stalks.
He knows what magic is.
The lightness of the skull he found
on the moor surprised him.
The roughened texture of the bone
that colour would destroy cried out
for coal.
The more he worked, the more
the crooked shadows drew him in
until he fell into the depths behind the
the hollow bones.
He saw then what the eyes
of innocence had seen – an ecstasy
of sunbeams, fields and meadows.
New-born lambs on springs at play
and coal black wings above.
Below, the shadows gathering.

187

WINTER SNOW

For many years, we had a family tradition that on New Year's Day, or as close to it as we could get, we would spend a day walking in the Lake District. When we began this ritual, we would go on January 1st whatever the weather, but gradually we became more circumspect and eventually gave up when work, other commitments, or a prolonged spell of rain forced us to delay our plans. However, January 3rd, 1987, had a good weather forecast and, because Brenda and I had seen the New Year in at a Keswick Hotel and were on our way home, we agreed to meet Kathryn at Dunmail Raise. She had seen the New Year in at Coniston Youth Hostel.

This was a spur of the moment decision, so it's not surprising that I hadn't got my ice axe. The tops were all snow covered but I knew, from the rain that had kept us in the hotel during some part of the previous days, that snow that had fallen overnight would be fresh and unconsolidated, although in places there might be a layer of ice underneath. Before Kathryn and I set off, I arranged with Brenda that we'd meet her at the King's Head at Thirlspot while I would lead Kathryn over Seat Sandal and Helvellyn.

This would turn out to be another day sent from heaven. It was cold and frosty, but the sun was reflecting diamonds in the fresh snow as we climbed to the top of Seat Sandal. From there with the sun behind us we could see others in the distance making their way up Dollywaggon Pike. There was no chance of us getting lost on such a day – not that there would have been, even on a bad day. My ice axe would have been a help but stopping to put crampons on would have been a hindrance. It was easy enough to kick steps where the snow had frozen to a thin crust and a real pleasure to find conditions there that we had seldom experienced before. There were serious climbers on the crags below the cornice that hung above Nethermost Cove. I kept us well away from the edge and did so all the way until we were beyond Hevellyn's summit. We were down at the King's Head to meet Brenda four hours after setting off.

188

The Helvellyn Range
January 3rd 1987

In February 1991, Kathryn and her husband, Peter, announced that they intended moving to Keswick to buy and run a B & B guest house. For me, this seemed a good idea – I'd taken early retirement in 1990, and in May 1992, Brenda would do the same. The guest house would be somewhere to stay close to the heart of the Lake District when, and if, trade was slack. Moreover, at busier times we could also earn our keep by helping with the washing and cleaning etc.

We were staying there in November 1992 when there was a heavy snowfall that covered the tops, although the roads were clear. Kathryn was keen to have a good walk and Brenda was happy to drive us, so I chose to start from the road between Crummock Water and Lanthwaite Green where a steep climb begins almost immediately. I'd driven past that side of Grasmoor many times and thought that it must be one of the longest, steepest, climbs in the whole of the Lake District. In fact, it climbs about 2,200 ft in a horizontal distance of half a mile or so. The strenuous

189

nature of the ascent was enough to keep us warm until we reached the summit where we were met by a bitterly cold east wind carrying bullets of frozen snow. The conditions on top were truly Arctic. I'd told Brenda that we'd meet her at the top of Whinlatter Pass in the visitor centre where she would be able to keep warm and buy herself a coffee. I'd intended to include Eel Crag and Sail but although we were both wearing thermals and were well wrapped up against the cold, Kathryn began to suffer from frozen fingers, so I decided it was better to make straight for Hopegill Head and Grizedale Pike. From there we dropped straight down to Whinlatter Forest and the visitor centre. I'm sure that, given the wind chill factor, it was one of the coldest days I've experienced on a Lake District mountain.

The weather was better the next day and I felt sure that the snow conditions would still be safe enough to climb Scafell from Wasdale. It's a long drive from Keswick to Wasdale but Brenda was happy to oblige again. As we drove the length of Wastwater, the Scafells, Lingmell, Kirkfell and Great Gable all looked magnificent under a blanket of snow that I estimated came down to about 1500 ft.

When Brenda and I had left Wigan for Keswick, I hadn't been expecting there to be any snow, so because I'd left my ice axe at home, I took Kathryn up a route to Scafell across Green How that kept us away from any danger and approached the summit from the south-west. Nobody else was up there, nor did we meet anybody all day, so we spent some time admiring the ice and snow-covered Pinnacle from the top of Deep Gill while keeping at a safe distance. The snow underfoot had developed a thin crust and we didn't encounter any ice, but I didn't intend taking any chances. Crampons, ice axes and a rope would have been necessary for any party attempting to climb Deep Gill under those conditions. My only mistake had been to leave my camera back at the house because the sun came out and the scene was transformed. Nevertheless, it was a day that has lived long in my memory.

190

ACCIDENTS WILL HAPPEN (2)

Recently, whenever we had a three-night stay in Borrowdale, Brenda and I had developed a mutual agreement that when returning home, I would have a run from Rosthwaite to either Grasmere or Langdale, while she would drive over Dunmail Raise to meet me. This worked well for many years at all times of day, all times of year, and in all weathers. However, as the years passed, the runs became jogs and eventually walks – at least on the uphill sections. In 2009, much to my chagrin, I became a mountain rescue statistic on my way to meet Brenda in Grasmere.

We'd enjoyed our three nights in Borrowdale and I'd had one good walk on a hot day over Melbreak from the Kirkstile Inn to Buttermere, memorable for finding a digital camera on the summit (which I handed in to the Keswick police), and also for unexpectedly coming across a scantily clad young woman bathing in the pool at the foot of Scale Force. I hope I behaved like a gentleman as I turned my back on her for a few minutes to admire a no less beautiful but equally alluring view of Crummock Water and Whiteless Pike.

Rain was falling the day we left for home, so we parked at Rosthwaite, waiting for it to ease off before I set off for Grasmere by way of Stonethwaite and Greenup Edge. I emphasise that I was not running nor, (I think) being careless, nor was I on a difficult rock-strewn path. In fact, the path was close to being horizontal. However, a little rain over the preceding days had left some damp stretches. I was within a couple miles of Grasmere when my foot slipped and I fell, landing on the only rock in the immediate area. I heard a distinct crack and found it impossible to stand, let alone walk, without excruciating pain. I knew I had a broken leg – actually my left femur, that would need a mountain rescue call out. Fortunately, the pain disappeared provided I didn't move and, fortunately again, that path is part of Wainwright's Coast to Coast route. I repeat, I was not running, although I had passed several walkers, who I knew would soon come across this fast walker now stranded on his back like one of the impotent black beetles that he'd known as a boy.

No sensible climber or fell walker goes into the hills without taking a number of precautions so I had my mobile phone with me (for emergency use only). Unfortunately, there was no signal where I'd fallen, and I had to wait for a Good Samaritan to come to my aid. Strangers are often exceedingly kind, so while an American couple doing Wainwright's coast to coast walk wrapped me in a shiny survival blanket, a young couple were able to contact the Langdale and Ambleside Mountain Rescue Team (LAMRT). They also contacted Brenda, who was driving over Dunmail Raise as usual, expecting to meet me in Grasmere. I was able to describe my location to LAMRT as being in Far Easedale and the recue team arrived about an hour or so later, having driven their Land Rover as far as Stythwaite Steps.

As soon as the rescue team arrived, I was given a morphine injection and my injured leg was immobilised for my transfer to a stretcher. I was also given gas and air which I was allowed to control. The efficiency of the rescue team impressed me greatly as I recalled everything I'd learnt in 1957 on the OBMS course where I'd acted as anchor man lowering a stretcher (with simulated casualty) down a rock face on Gowbarrow Crag.

Because of the morphine I was only semi-conscious during the rescue, but I was aware all the time of the communication between my bearers as they carried me down to the rescue vehicle – 'boggy bit', 'mind the rock', 'big step down' etc. At the LAMRT headquarters I was transferred to an ambulance and taken to Lancaster Hospital. Brenda, meanwhile, had driven as far towards Easedale as possible and followed the ambulance to Lancaster. I was released from hospital after 7 days. The LAMRT report in the Westmorland Gazette ended with words which I like to think exonerate me from any stupidity, 'He was just unlucky.' For the benefit of any medically inclined readers, the official report describes the damage as "an intracapsular fracture of L. neck of femur repaired by a left hip corial hemiarthroplasty, bipolar". The operation to replace the head of the femur is the subject of the next poem.

Far Easedale from the slopes of Helm Crag.
The accident occurred where the hanging valley at the centre of
the picture curves down to the left.
Photo taken ten years later on March 26th 2019

Theatre

The performance I have to admit
was a huge success which is not
to say it was enjoyable, being interrupted
at intervals by demons who sang
discordant songs before an eyeballed
maelstrom of swirling colours
which they told me later was
due to the diamorphine,

there being no other drug with sufficient
power to mask the pain of the saw used
to decapitate at the neck the head of the
left femur replacing it with an anvil chorus
of hammers tapping the titanium ball and
pin into their correct alignment.

But it was an undoubted success for
I have since climbed a mountain or two,
although I'll never run another marathon.

MAGIC MOMENTS

For all the apparent toil and trouble that goes into training, there are compensations, some of which occur unexpectedly. Who but another runner can understand the immense pleasure that one gets from encountering a large party ascending, let's say, the steep path to Loughrigg Fell from Grasmere? You have already spent a happy hour or two covering a few miles of your training run and are starting to feel totally drained on your way back to your car, parked in the village. But now that it's downhill you are relaxed and moving well.

Then you meet the party on the narrow path and their leader gives a shout, '*Make way. Fit people coming,*' and with that commendation ringing in your ears you develop wings on your heels, and you fly past them like a messenger from the gods with a brief '*Thank you*'. Of course, they don't know about the shortage of breath you had on the ascent, or the pain in your hips from your developing arthritis, or the pills you take every day for half a dozen ailments. But that mention of "fit people" did you a power of good and you vow you'll carry on however hard it becomes.

A somewhat similar incident occurred during a road race before I even considered fell running. I was running at a nice easy pace in a road race with Kathryn (who may not relish this account) when a young stranger caught up with us. I let the two of them draw away from me for a while until I saw him leave her and she slowed down to allow me to catch her up. I was very much gratified when she explained that he'd obviously been chatting her up and had asked her if I was her husband or her boyfriend!

I have never entered a fell race expecting to win anything, but in 1984 when, looking back, I suppose I was as fit as I was ever likely to be, I entered the Duddon Fell race. This is classed as an "A" Long race, in this case, 20 miles and 6,000 ft of climbing, so it's not one to be undertaken lightly. Somehow, that year the race had not been listed in the FRA race calendar. Furthermore, heavy rain was falling in Wigan on the morning of the race day, and I nearly decided not to bother going, but I'd registered my entry in advance and was keen. Brenda was happy to drive herself to the coast or go for a walk somewhere while I disappeared into the hills for about five hours.

When we arrived at the Newfield Inn in the Duddon Valley, the rain had stopped and the clouds were dispersing. I went to let the organisers know I was there and heard one of them remark. *'Oh, good, we've got a race.'* I didn't understand what she meant but thought no more about it. The eight check points that need to be visited *en route* effectively delineate the Duddon valley skyline – Harter Fell, Hardknott Fell, Little Stand, Three Shire Stone, Swirl How, Dow Crag. White Pike and Caw.

Only 31 runners had turned up for the start and, within five minutes of setting off, having crossed the intake fields from the Newfield Inn to where the route turns by the River Duddon, all the other runners had left me behind. I was alone, but the rain had stopped and the sun had come out, so I decided I might as well settle down to enjoy a long day out at a comfortable pace.

When I emerged from the small gorge where the river Duddon runs below Wallowbarrow Crag I could see the others ahead of me, now beginning to spread out, but once they entered the forest at Grassguards, they disappeared again and after that I saw nobody all day except the marshals at the various check points. It was now a matter of not getting lost and finding the checkpoints although I was so far behind the others that I no longer thought of it as a race. However, I continued to move as fast as I could, while still enjoying the sensation of speed without getting too much out of breath. I even stopped briefly to exchange a few words with some of the marshals.

I think it was at the penultimate check point on White Pike that the marshals asked me if I'd seen a couple of other runners. I had to tell them, 'Sorry but I've seen nobody at all since the start.' That was my first intimation that I might not be last, so it spurred me on to try harder although at that stage I was suffering from cramp and dehydration. What had so far been a relaxed and enjoyable day out now become a desperate desire not to disgrace myself by being last.

196

I reached the final check point on Caw and half walked and half ran down the mountain to the finish line. But I was so terribly thirsty that I needed a drink and was within sight of the finish when I came to a stream. I took a quick glance behind to ensure that nobody was about to pass me and scooped up a few mouthfuls of crystal clear, cool refreshing spring water.

Three minutes later, I crossed the finish line to the sound of clapping. I was taken by the arm to the presentation table where the comment made by the registration marshal at the start about there being a race became clear. There were only two entries in the "Supervet" category that day and, being the first one to finish, I received a glass tankard engraved with an outline of the race route and the legend *Duddon Fell Race 1984 – 1st*. What more could any fell runner hope for.

The Chevy Chase, a "B Long" fell race at 20 miles and 4,000ft, starts from the youth hostel at Wooler as related earlier. Brenda and I were still YHA members, so it was a useful venue for us to have a weekend away. Brenda could explore the local villages, castles and historic sites while I disappeared as usual into the distant wilds of Cheviot and Hedgehope, two hills close to the northern end of the Pennine Way.

I first entered the race in 1990 and had such happy memories that it became one of my favourite races and I continued to enter every year until 2002. Much like the London Marathon there were then, in effect, three separate races – one for walkers, one for slow runners and one for "elite" runners. The start times were staggered to avoid the marshals having to be out on the hills for too long. That first race was memorable for the ceilidh in the hostel that evening after the race. Never before had I enjoyed so much beer to the sound of a folk band that included a skilful young girl playing the Northumbrian pipes. It was an evening of pure magic.

Sadly, such an evening hasn't happened since, but there have been compensations at the hostel after the race with evening talks on subjects as varied as local wild-life, geology and the history of the area. One year, the race organiser, Lawrence Heslop, arranged a field trip to visit cup and ring marks carved on rocks on private

197

land, not accessible except by permission of the landowner. On another occasion Lawrence allowed me the privilege of blowing the whistle (or was it sounding the horn) to signal the start of the walkers' race.

During one race I noticed that three runners ahead of me had stopped. I thought it was a strange thing to do but when I reached them, I understood, and I also had to pause. There are more important things in life than getting to the end of a race as quickly as possible. They had come across an adder coiled on a sun warmed rock, blissfully unaware of our presence. If only one of us had taken a camera!

Snake

Racing down the hill we suddenly
stopped. A snake was sleeping
unconcerned, as if nobody
ever came that way. Spirally coiled
she had gathered for herself
the sun-soaked comfort of a stone.
The diamond scales were proof
of what she was, but no one moved,
nor dared disturb her innocence.
This was a privilege so rarely seen.
On such a sun-blessed day no runner
hoping for a personal best
would stop to look.

Nobody racing thinks to stop.
But maybe stops to think.
And so, we did.
For in that moment, time
itself had stopped for us.

STAC POLLY aka STAC POLLAIDH or AN STAC

Stac Polly is a mountain that bursts upon the sight suddenly when seen from the A835 climbing out of Ullapool towards Kylesku. Standing at a height of a mere 2,011 ft, Stac Polly hardly merits the appellation of mountain; it is a dwarf among giants, a child among adults, but like a child it has a charming simplicity.

Stac Pollaidh from the A 835 roadside
June 1989

The rock formations, including one known as "The Lobster's Claw", are unrivalled by any others throughout the kingdom and may be examined at close range by walking around Stac Polly's base. I know of no other hill that can give so much enjoyment from so little expenditure of energy – the summit is only a mile or so from the roadside car park.

The ascent begins as soon as you close the car door and a fit young walker could be up and down well inside a couple of hours. But why rush about when there is so much to cherish? No sane person would think to spend so little time on so perfect a hill.

For a start, there are two distinct summits at opposite ends of a connecting saddle, perhaps half a mile in length. The eastern summit can be reached easily enough but the western top, which is the highest point, requires more determination, a steady nerve and a head for heights. Having spent the night at Ullapool Youth Hostel, I climbed it with Brenda on a cloudless, windless day in June 1989, when several cars were already parked by the roadside. The rough, rocky terrain of the higher reaches were not to Brenda's liking, so she was happy to rest at the saddle with Sam, our little mongrel terrier. I polished off the lesser top very quickly without any trouble and returned to sit for a while and share a drink with Brenda before heading west to complete the climb.

I knew before I began that I would need to conquer a short rock climb if I were to succeed. The track was easy enough to follow amongst the rocky debris that littered the saddle leading up to the western summit until I reached the climb that would possibly deter many walkers from proceeding further. My first impression, seen from a distance as I approached, was that there would be no problem, but closer inspection revealed that the holds, such as they were, sloped outwards. The absence of any "jug handles" meant that hand and foothold safety would depend mostly on friction against the rock. I could see only one route up that steep, though short, rock face that might, as rock climbers say, "go". Moreover, there appeared to be a vertical drop of about two hundred feet immediately below it. Even more worrying was the thought that, having attained the summit, I would have to descend by the same route. I withdrew for a while to get a better view and sat down to examine the climb, short though it was. I wanted to plan every step (they were few) and was trying to summon up the courage I needed to continue.

'Are you going to sit there all day?' a woman already sitting nearby enquired. For a moment I wondered if she was waiting, perhaps even hoping, for some unfortunate adventurer to take a tumble.

'My husband's already up there,' she told me. 'He said it's not as hard as it looks'.

That decided me. Most fear lies in the anticipation of events that may never happen and five minutes later I was chatting to her husband on the summit. The return to the saddle needed only a modicum of extra care as I descended facing the rock. I was conscious, as I walked back along the length of the saddle, of another mountain far away to the north. But Suilven would have to wait for thirty years, during which time I have always thought of Stac Polly as being "Son of Suilven". Go one day and experience its delights for yourself.

Suilven on the left and Canisp
from the path on Stac Pollaidh saddle,
June 1989

LIATHACH

By June 1989, I had been back in England for less than a year after spending twelve months working in India. I had little opportunity abroad to maintain my fitness level owing to 1) the hours spent working, which were effectively from dawn to dusk six days a week, and 2) the heat that caused anyone moving at anything faster than a brisk walk to break into a serious sweat. I never went any distance without carrying two litres of water, and on one cycle ride, even that was barely sufficient. But I wanted to get back to some real mountains, so we went again to Scotland's west coast, making use of several youth hostels.

We had two nights at Ullapool Y.H. before moving on to Lochinver. It was during this short drive that we climbed Stac Polly (described above). We booked ahead for Durness and the day was so good that I persuaded Brenda to drop me off along the road by Quinag, where I would do a quick "up and down". I would meet her a couple of miles or so further on. The weather at Durness was incredibly hot so far north so we spent a day by Smoo Cave relaxing in the sun and I had a swim in the North Sea. A cold sea mist (haar) enveloped the coast the next day, so we returned to Torridon Y.H. From there I was near enough to spend a day on Liathach – one of the finest ridge walks on the Scottish mainland. Sadly, it was a day of low cloud and mist. Brenda dropped me off at 9.00am on the A896 in Glen Torridon and an hour later I was on the ridge but could see nothing of the majestic cliffs and mighty corries for which the mountain is famed.

The climb was simple enough, although very steep and involved a series of horizontal strata interspersed with patches of scree and grass. There was a deep gully to my left for most of the way, but not so much as to create a feeling of danger. I knew the ridge extended further to the east so once I reached it, I turned right and followed it eastward as far as a steep descent where the mist thinned. From there I could see nothing but space beyond, so I returned along the ridge, now heading west, to climb to the summit of Spidean a'Choire Leith where I rested and ate my lunch.

There, I was surrounded by nothing but impenetrable mist, but I soon noticed a ptarmigan that seemed to look at me suspiciously. I watched it walking from side to side, occasionally disappearing behind the rocks that littered the summit. Was it hoping for me to throw it a crumb or two, or was I sitting too close to its nest? I knew there was an exciting ridge to come so I didn't linger and after scattering a peace offering of crumbs, I left the ptarmigan in its mountain fastness.

Ptarmigan on Liathach
June 1989

I began the traverse of the Am Fasarinen Ridge by trying to stay as high as possible and climb all the pinnacles. All was going well until I reached a point where I decided it would be too dangerous for me to continue, being so high above a path that I knew skirted the more difficult sections, so I dropped down to it. After following the path for a short distance, I had a strange sensation that all was not right and got my compass out. I hadn't thought it would be necessary on such a sharp ridge, but I realised I was now walking east, not west. The ups and downs of the pinnacles with their associated twists and turns had completely reversed my sense of direction.

Beyond the end of the Am Fasarinen Ridge, the climb up to Liathach's western peak of Mullach an Rathain follows an easy path and I raced along it, stopping at times to look back hoping that the eastern peak would emerge from the clouds. Sadly, it never did, and I was at sea level by Loch Torridon, having made a slow and frustrating descent by the abominable stone shoot, before the full length of Liathach became visible.

Looking back to Spidean a' Choire Leith
from Mullach an Rathain, Liathach
June 1989

Sundew

On famined moors the deadly
eye-lashed sundew offers
nectar to the unsuspecting fly.
And I, twelve months of hungering
for another hill, would rather die
than miss this crumbling Clisham*
tempting me.

Though well-worn paths pave
Sassenach fells, here
lies a wild untrodden land,
of steep, unstable, shattered scree
deceptively designed to ambush
careless feet on tilted stones.

Returning from the hill, a valley cut
by centuries of rainstorm bars the way,
and on its brink between my feet, I spy
a pennyworth of sundew ringed by tears.
More dangerous than the mountain lives
this golden eye, its dewy lashes glistening
here like pearls below my bloodied shins.

*The Clisham is the highest point of the Outer Hebrides

*Outer Hebrides, The Clisham from the roadside
June 4th 2008*

Blue Grass

What did I know of space?
I, who viewed the world
from mountain tops
never understood your fear of lifts,
your preference for stairs, your grief
at finding claustrophobia
on the sixteenth floor.

I've watched them change
the sheets. Replace the pillow.
Pull back the curtains.
Let in the light.
But I still sit. Behind
my eyes one memory fills
the space in which you
told me I'd survive.
The place you occupied is
free to wander now from
room to room not using doors.
But here some atoms of the air
you breathed must still be mingling,
silent with my own. Carbolic fills
the space left by the Blue Grass
from your perfume spray.
As insubstantial as the catalogue
of dreams we never opened.

LIFE AFTER DEATH

By the summer of 2015 it was time to find out if I could book a single room at the Borrowdale Hotel without suffering the pangs of bereavement. Brenda had died in April the previous year and I had decided before then that I would leave her ashes on top of Pendle Hill, because that was the first hill of any size that we had climbed together without being accompanied by one or more friends. [See page 49.] It would also be a challenge to my advanced years and at the same time be somewhere close enough to visit from home whenever I felt inclined. The year before would have been too soon for comfort and in any case, I had many details to attend to for several weeks after the funeral. I was also adjusting my life to living alone.

On June 1st 2015, I drove to Keswick and chose, for nostalgic OBMS reasons, George Fisher's climbing shop from amongst the plethora of other shops there, to buy a new haversack. But I eschewed walking shoes on account of their cost and found a comfortable, cheaper pair elsewhere the next day. While there, I drove to Whitehaven to visit Grace, an old friend (in both senses) of mine and Brenda's. It was a welcome visit and between us we recalled other visits that Brenda and I had made to her over the preceding fifty or so years.

The next day I made good use of my Keswick purchases by driving to Seathwaite, where I left the car, intending to climb Scafell Pike. This was partly to test my fitness but would also be a precursor to my projected visit to Scotland to fulfil a long-held ambition to traverse the ridge of An Teallach. I realised almost as soon as I left the car that it was going to be a hard day. By the time I crossed the river at Stockley Bridge, the pain from my left femur, broken six years previously, had become noticeable though not so much as to stop me from going on, and I reached Styhead in an hour and fifteen minutes with rather more puffing and panting than in my youth. The higher ground was in cloud, but I knew, or thought I knew, the route to the start of the Corridor route. I couldn't see a path where I'd expected to find one, so I set off towards Esk Hause before branching off to the right. I was almost correct and soon picked up a narrow path. In any case the direct line that I half remembered (and is favoured by fell runners) crosses a depression that would have been too wet and muddy for my lovely new shoes.

Once on the path, the way remained clear enough until I climbed into cloud at around 2,500 ft. I was now trying to recall the many twists and turns, the many ups and downs and the ins and outs of that fascinating path that crosses the top of the infamous Piers Gill. Two hours from Styhead I reached the summit where I found a dozen or so people enjoying lunch. I chose a suitable rock as a seat to rest my painful hip, meanwhile chatting to a visitor from Wisconsin. He also was alone, but younger, and so not surprisingly faster than me, and had passed me on the ascent. It would probably be his only visit there and I felt sorry for him not being able to enjoy the views that I knew so well. Every glorious view was obscured by the all-enveloping cloud.

When I set off again, I realised I was much less sure of my balance so, on the rocky terrain that I once used to run across, I now went slowly ensuring that I didn't fall and break my other femur. I was heading for Esk Hause and found the path over Broad Crag and Ill Crag to be much rougher than I remembered, so my progress was very slow indeed. However, before reaching Esk Hause, in my best fell-running style, I cut off a corner by descending from Calf Cove on Great End straight to the top of Ruddy Gill.

Descending then by Ruddy Gill was a sore trial for I needed to stop several times to ease the pain that had increased and was starting to exacerbate my balance problems. At one point I had to swallow my pride when a party that I'd been trying to keep behind me, caught me up and I had to allow them past. As they did so, for a moment I wished I could return to those glorious days when I rejoiced in the exhilaration of speed, but I soon came down to earth with the thought that those memories will last as long as I live. Once in sight of Cockley Bridge, I turned aside to sit quietly alone a few yards from the path, enjoy a drink and watch other walkers descending. One party carrying large rucksacks was ascending and being so late in the day, I guessed their purpose. I called out to them to ask and found that I was right. How I envied them their intention to spend a night or two of wild camping and, hopefully, enjoy the sunrise from a chosen summit. I was soon down after that and much relieved to be walking with less pain on relatively horizontal ground. Despite the pain, it had been a good day that I finished with a soak in a hot bath and an excellent evening meal.

Looking from Calf Cove to the head of Ruddy Gill
June 3rd 2015

The next day, as I expected, my left ankle had seized up, being the legacy of the sprain sustained during my OBMS days. Troutdale isn't too far from the hotel for an injured enthusiast to walk into, so I set off on a perfect morning to do just that, expecting to return the same way.

Once in the quiet secluded vale where few people go, other than climbers bound for Black Crag, I walked a little way up the dry bracken-clad slope facing the crag and sat down to enjoy the perfect peace and the view of Skiddaw beyond Derwentwater. There was no wind, and the only sign of life was a buzzard circling high above. Nor was there any sound except for the twittering background of a multitude of small birds, broken only by the occasional calls of a cuckoo and a woodpecker somewhere in the distant woods across the valley.

Happily, I was moving more freely when I stood up, so instead of returning directly to the hotel, I continued by the roadside to Grange where I added a postscript to my poem of September 2013, which I'd left in the now closed Methodist church at Grange where Brenda and I had worshipped during our honeymoon fifty-six years earlier in 1959. I finished my short morning walk by completing the round trip back to the hotel from Manesty taking the well-known path that uses the "Chinese" bridge to cross the river.

Troutdale
June 4ᵗʰ 2015

Holiness Unwritten

There is space on every mountain
only known to those who look,
and the empty desert landscape
is a holy, unread book,

and the midnight sky that stretches
to the very edge of space
is ablaze with unseen glory
from our God of love and grace.

When a Schubert quintet pauses
and the notes hang on a prayer,
in the silence of that moment
you will know that God is there.

In the hollowed bowls of tulips
lies a heaven worth more than gold,
and the empty nests of skylarks
tell of joy they cannot hold.

You may glory in church windows,
in the glass stained blue or green,
but God's love is also painted
on the bare walls in-between.

Such places are the spaces
on a half-completed chart.
They are holiness unwritten
on the pages of your heart.

September 2013

A RIDGE TOO FAR

Echoing the words of Sir Edmund Hillary after he climbed Everest with Sherpa Tenzing, I would like to say that "we knocked the bastard off". But I can't because we didn't. My reason for travelling to the far North-West of Scotland was not to climb An Teallach, arguably the finest, hardest and most spectacular mountain ridge on the British mainland, but to find out if, at the age of seventy-nine, I could. Well, the simple answer is – I couldn't. I must remind you at the outset that I have climbed many mountains, so I was expecting the climb to be a challenge. Also, fearing for my safety, Rosalind insisted on accompanying me.

Our climb began immediately from the roadside where we parked the car and we progressed upwards pleasantly enough through birch woods to the sound of a woodpecker hammering away and a stream that chattered to itself merrily alongside the path. Having climbed about a thousand feet, we reached a large cairn from where a secondary path crosses moorland and drops down to a mountain refuge, the Shenavall Bothy. We were to pass this bothy several hours later.

Although five minutes behind my schedule, it was a good place for me to rest before we began the ascent of a steepening gradient towards the subsidiary peak of Sail Liath which towered above us for another two thousand feet. The upper slopes were, to say the least, difficult, being composed of unstable and almost pathless shattered scree. My age was already beginning to tell and by the time we reached a suitable place for lunch, we were an hour behind schedule. From the summit of Sail Liath we had our first sight of the awesome obstacle to come – a curving ridge that resembled the spine of a giant Stegosaurus. Our prospects of success, I thought to myself were not good, for once committed to the main ridge, there would be no escape to either side.

From Sail Liath, we dropped to a col, regretting the loss of much hard-earned height, and then had to climb again to Stob Cadha Gobhlach, the next peak along the ridge. In the Lake

District, both would count as separate peaks, but here on An Teallach, they hardly merit a mention. We now dropped again before another climb, this time towards the "bad step" where purists wishing to follow the ridge in its entirety rope up. Fortunately, for the faint hearted there is a convenient path below this obstacle which we took, hoping to return to the main ridge further on. That is to say, we followed the path as far as a corner beyond which the ground fell away so steeply that to continue in my condition would have been folly.

My legs had turned to jelly, the titanium implant in my left hip was giving me hell, and my daughter was concerned, not only for me, but also for her own safety. We held a conference and decided to return to the last col below the "bad step". There, faced with either retracing our route which involved climbing back over two summits and descending through the abominable scree of Sail Liath, or dropping down the easier looking southern slopes to Loch na Sealga at sea level, I made a decision which, with the advantage of hindsight, was the wrong one.

That mountainside was not as innocuous as it appeared. The ground was at first easy, consisting of gently sloping, almost (for myself as a fit, young fell runner) runnable scree interspersed with small grassy oases. Thankfully, a few rocky outcrops that had been invisible from above, owing to the convex nature of the ground, could be turned easily enough. The major problem was that, as we continued to descend, heather began to proliferate and, in so doing, hid the underlying terrain. For the last thousand feet of the descent, each step required a careful test of the cushioning vegetation to determine what lay beneath. We seldom felt the assurance of solid ground, and the frequent need to adjust my balance drained me of whatever energy I still had. Furthermore, it was impossible to rest amongst the heather owing to the swarms of midges that were released. When we reached the loch, I had no strength whatsoever left in my legs. By the shore I sat on a rock and consumed a whole tin of rice pudding, carried for the very purpose of providing a slow energy release for the final hours of the day.

Our car was still a good six miles away on the far side of the moorland mentioned above that would require us to climb and drop another thousand feet. There was no path by the loch, but we soon reached a thankfully dry, but narrow path that led us to the Shenavall Bothy an hour later. From there the final climb of the day began and I filled my water bottle frequently whenever I could. The twists and turns of the indistinct path across the moor were not a problem, although I still needed frequent stops to rest. At last, the cairn where I had rested earlier came into view and with it the relief that the rest of the day would be downhill. When we reached the car, we had been on our feet for over twelve hours. For an aged semi-invalid, An Teallach had proved to be a ridge too far. Although it had been a day of undoubted hardship, I felt a delightful sense of achievement – and I had my answer. It is better to have tried and failed than never to have tried at all.

The forbidding rocky ridge of An Teallach
as seen from Cadha Gobhlach on the failed ascent
May 2016

ON TURNING EIGHTY

Perception of age is very much like a moveable, or perhaps I should say, an educational feast. Up to the age of ten, thinking about the future is of little concern to anyone. Children live in the present; they take no thought for whatever lies in wait for them. They know that Christmas will come eventually, but today they have a game to play, food will appear as if by magic and tomorrow can wait. For children, time will last forever and should, by chance, a fleeting thought of time invade their minds, it's soon dismissed. Time, if they ever think about it, stretches far away to disappear inside a mystical and undiscovered haze that has no bearing on the present. Time is a word without meaning, even though they are told that to save it is a virtue and to waste it a sin. Despite these exhortations, and although subject to certain restraints such as school, and possibly medical needs, they are mostly at liberty to spend their time how they will.

But when, for the first time their age becomes a double digit, there is a concomitant, though admittedly still little understood, realisation that they have entered another world, a feeling made more forcefully when, so soon afterwards, they become a pubescent teenager. The attractions of the adult world begin to beckon and can't come soon enough. By then, the mists are beginning imperceptibly to thin a little, although the thought that time is passing and cannot be denied is quickly pushed aside and forgotten. However, hopes begin to crystallize, ideas take shape, decisions are made, and dreams and hopes for what might lie ahead become a possibility.

One by one, the decades come and go, each one being recognised as something special. Too old at forty? Doesn't life begin at forty? When you wave your bat to the pavilion at fifty, you suddenly realise you're probably over half-way to the grave. If you're lucky, you retire at sixty, or even earlier. Then you reach your threescore years and ten and you rejoice, remembering with sadness the friends you knew who didn't make it so far. But you also realise that the rites of passage, the milestones and the decades have been flickering past at an ever-increasing rate and the years left to you are fewer than you thought. That's when you go into your mental stock room where you find a pile of faded, dusty memories to rummage through. And that's when, before it's too late, you wonder how to celebrate your next big birthday.

Approaching my 80th birthday, I wanted it to be different from all those that had gone before. For our major birthdays Brenda and I, being born in the same year, usually arranged, in addition to any other annual holiday, to go for a weekend away in a plush hotel in both April and June. But Brenda had died before her 77th birthday and I didn't see any point in celebrating my 80th birthday alone, even at our favourite Borrowdale Hotel. After considering several options, I decided I would like to take my close family on a walk that would give them something to remember. I arranged for Rosalind, Kathryn and Peter, and my brother, Peter. and his wife Shân, to join me for a few days at the Borrowdale Hotel. In the event my two nieces, Cerian and Heather, and their partners, Ben and Roger, came as well, together with Emilia, my great niece, aged one, the most recent and, therefore, the youngest addition to the family.

I thought that the Gable Girdle would be a good walk, (there are no summits involved). But knowing the state of my left hip and ankle that had been sorely tried on An Teallach the previous year, I needed to try it out first. So, in May 2017 I booked three nights at the Borrowdale Hotel. I had climbed Great Gable with Brenda on our honeymoon and had done so (alone) many times since, so I was hoping that a circuit of the mountain without visiting the summit would not be too taxing.

But I was mistaken, although for six hours or so, the concentration required allowed me (almost) to forget the Manchester bomb tragedy that had occurred two days earlier. I drove to Seathwaite to save a couple of miles of road walking and didn't use the usual path to Styhead. I wanted a good view of Taylor Ghyll Waterfall, which is seen better from the western bank of the stream issuing from Styhead Tarn than from the popular path. But this path seemed much more eroded than when I'd once used it on a previous occasion – in fact it was so long ago that I couldn't remember. When I checked later, I found it was in 1960. This time, the climb up the steep slopes alongside the fall was distinctly hairy in places. If I were to bring the family, I would have to take them by the standard tourist route on the far bank.

Ennerdale from below Gable Crag
May 2017

The top of Styhead Pass is where the Girdle begins in earnest, although the first section is an easy rising walk to the base of Kern Knotts Buttress. From there the track became very indistinct in places, especially where it crossed any scree (there's a lot of scree) and I had to take care to watch where I was placing my feet. I knew that my balance was no longer that of a young man. At one point I had to rest for a couple of minutes to consider the best way to descend a short but near vertical slab. Sixty years ago I wouldn't even have slowed down. Below the Napes Ridges there was more rock than scree, but care was still necessary. I could hear the voices of climbers above me, possibly on Napes Needle. How I envied them as I thought of how I once explored those crags alone. At Beckhead I sat out of the wind for lunch before continuing the traverse below Gable Crag, from where I took a photograph. The climb to Windy Gap that followed was on unstable, slippery scree, And painful. My left hip was even more painful during the descent as I returned to Styhead, and from there I had to rest twice more before I reached Seathwaite. It had been a superb walk, taking six hours with many rests, but I would have to arrange something easier on my birthday for a party of eleven people and a dog.

The next day my ankle had seized up as it usually did, but it gradually eased off and by mid-morning I reckoned I could manage a trial walk of a few miles, so I was waiting for the 10.35 bus to Rosthwaite when I got into conversation with three ladies. They were also staying at the hotel and planned to walk through Ashness Woods to Watendlath and return by way of Rosthwaite. I told them that I intended to take the bus to Rosthwaite and return by way of Dock Tarn, Watendlath and Ashness Woods, so there was a possibility we might meet. My plan would take in country that was new to me, despite the many weekends and short breaks that I'd spent in the area with Brenda.

Rather than take the road to Stonethwaite, I chose the rough path on the true right bank of Stonethwaite Beck and ambled along enjoying the warmth of the sun while listening to the distant bleating of new-born lambs. There's a steep climb through woods to the plateau that contains Dock Tarn, but it consists mostly of carefully placed steps, and while I'm not usually in favour of such human interference with nature, here I was thankful for the relief the steps gave to my aching hip.

Once on less demanding ground, the winding path is bounded by heather as far as the tarn where the main path to Watendlath follows the shore. At that point a minor path strikes off uphill to the left, and as I was on new ground, I followed it for a short distance until it disappeared amongst a wilderness of bogs. Eventually it would lead one to the summit of Great Crag but for once, a summit was not my objective, so I returned to Dock Tarn to follow the delightful twists and turns of the path along the shore.

I was soon down at Watendlath where I found a pleasant patch of grass above the Churn to rest and eat my lunch. The sun was high in the sky then and occasionally I could hear the voices of walkers on the path behind me. I'd been lying down with my day sack for a pillow with my eyes closed and was half asleep when I heard voices that I recognised. I was surprised that the three ladies had taken so long but I didn't turn round, and they didn't see me. I learned that evening that they'd been lost in Ashness Woods, but I assured them that it was no disgrace, having once been lost there myself. Back at the hotel, I decided that it would be a much more suitable walk for my birthday than the Gable Girdle.

A month later, everyone arrived safely at the Borrowdale hotel, and on June 24th, we set off to walk the half-mile along the road to Grange. I wanted as little road walking as possible, so we crossed the double bridge at Grange to walk to Rosthwaite by the River Derwent below Castle Crag. There were a few minor diversions to explore caves and quarries *en route* and for Sophie (the golden retriever) to enjoy cooling herself in the river. At Rosthwaite we crossed over the bridge and turned right to follow the same path to Stonethwaite that I'd used earlier. Once we'd started the climb, we soon became spread out, the younger and fitter members of my party leading the way to the top of the steps, where they halted to wait for the rest of us. We were now well above the trees and were rewarded with glorious views of Eagle Crag and Glaramara. It was a perfect place to have our lunch on a day almost as sunny as the day I did my reconnoitre.

Going past Dock Tarn, some of the younger ones took the higher path on Great Crag and met us lower down on the Watendlath track. At Watendlath, we split again into two parties, both Peters, Cerian, Shân and I walking along the road to meet the others, who'd taken the footpath on the far side of the river, at the edge of Ashness woods. The path down through the woods reaches the road a mere two hundred yards from the hotel, so we were in the hotel by mid-afternoon with time to relax in the hotel garden with a selection of drinks from the bar. That evening we shared dinner and a birthday cake at a table decorated with balloons and sprinkled with sparkling 80s confetti.

Two days later, I was wakened by daylight streaming into my bedroom and I could see that the far side of the valley was in full sunshine. It was a morning too fine to stay in bed with so many options for an early walk, so I dressed in T-shirt, shorts and trainers and was away from the hotel by 6.00am. I was on top of Catbells an hour later with the hill to myself.

The summit of Catbells
7.00 am June 26th 2017

Dressed as I was, I'd felt colder than I'd expected as I crossed the valley. The sun hadn't risen far enough to reach the pastures,

221

even on the far side, so they were still in shade. Because of my left hip I couldn't even run to get warm, but once I began the climb and was in direct sunlight, I soon warmed up. Being alone on Catbells on such a morning was as good an experience as anyone could wish for, and as good a place as anyone could wish to be. By the time I left the summit the sun had reached the valley floor, and although I descended slowly and carefully, I was back at the hotel by 8.00am with, not surprisingly, an aching left hip.

For the rest of the day we took our visitors to see the Bowder Stone before they left for home. Rosalind, Kathryn, Peter and I then drove to the top of Gale Road to walk up Latrigg so that Kathryn and Peter could look down on Keswick and remember their days living there, while picking out various landmarks before they returned to New Zealand. I'd had a birthday to savour.

STORM ALI

I guess there comes a time in your life when you realise that you may never accomplish everything on your bucket list. By September 2018, I was fretting that I still hadn't climbed anything that year. But I had already booked three nights in Borrowdale so there would still be two full days to have a chance of adding to my memories. Unfortunately, those days happened to coincide with the arrival of storm Ali, a violent tempest that would add to the misery of Lakeland farmers and many others who were already suffering from previous inundations. However, I was determined to climb something.

The first full day was windy with driving rain, but I boarded the service bus to Seatoller, intending, despite the weather, to traverse Glaramara, last climbed the previous January with Rosalind and Adrian on a day of cloudless blue when anyone might have sunbathed, hoping to develop an enviable tan amongst the summit snow. [See page 228.] The contrast between then and my proposed ascent could not have been greater.

At around fifteen hundred feet I was bitterly cold and soaked to the skin. I knew the potential danger of hypothermia, especially for one so old and alone, so I retreated to enjoy a long soak in a hot bath. The weather that day was merely the prelude to the arrival of the full storm the next day. But I was not to be deterred. The forecast was for gale force winds at sea level, but there would be no more than a few showers.

Knowing that the wind would be generally from the south-west, I decided that it would be feasible to take the bus to Rosthwaite and traverse High Spy and Maiden Moor as far as Catbells. I supposed, correctly as it turned out, that the ridge itself would shield me from the worst of the gale during my ascent through Rigg Head quarries, and that once on the ridge, the wind would be mostly behind me.

The strength of the wind was apparent as soon as I stepped off the bus, but it was nothing compared to that which I would meet later. Trees alongside the Rosthwaite farm lane were bent to seemingly impossible angles by the gale and were struggling to stay upright. Twigs and leaves flew past, propelled by the wind with the speed of a swooping peregrine falcon. The stepping-stones at the end of the lane were submerged beneath a raging River Derwent, so I had to use the bridge. Two young lads who were repairing the wooden footbridge over Tongue Gill kindly stopped work for a moment to let me pass. I thought they were heroes to be working in such weather.

As I expected, the ascent through the quarries was easy enough, being sheltered with enough places to find occasional relief out of the wind. Once on the ridge though, with nothing to hinder it, the gale blew with, for me, an unprecedented ferocity, although when I think back, it may have been no stronger than when I once crossed Styhead on hands and knees, holding on to tussocks of grass during a Borrowdale fell race.

The noise that resembled an express locomotive, combined with the incessant flapping of my cagoule hood, was something that I remembered reading about in descriptions by Everest writers of spending nights on the South Col at around 27,000 feet. I was frequently forced to stop, and where the strength of the wind increased as it channelled through gaps between rocky outcrops, I had to drop to my hands and knees. Forward progress was of necessity slow, even with a following wind, and the effort needed to resist being blown over was surprisingly tiring. Every step required a conscious effort of will to ensure that my balance was secure with both my feet firmly planted before I could take the next step.

Once past the summit of High Spy, there seemed to be no point in continuing any further along the ridge under such conditions, so I abandoned my plan to stay on the ridge as far as Catbells. At a small depression, I dropped below the ridge on the Borrowdale side and followed a lower line where the wind, although still threatening to blow me over, was less violent.

On the other hand, where the wind on the ridge had been reasonably constant, now it came in unexpected gusts interspersed with periods of relative calm as if it were gathering itself for a further violent onslaught. I was particularly careful at all times to ensure that if I were blown over, there would be no rocks nearby on which I might land. After perhaps an hour of such travel, I had dropped far enough to find shelter behind an outcrop and eat a frugal lunch.

By then, the rain showers that from time to time had spattered on my cagoule hood had ceased and no longer stung my bare hands, which for the most part had been stretched out before me by the strength of the wind that had lifted my arms almost horizontally as I leant back against it. I was now facing a shallow grassy depression and was fascinated by watching the progress of the wind as it constantly changed direction, made visible by swathes of grass that waved, first one way and then another. After a while, although I was well away from any recognised path, I thought I could see, in the depression below the safety of my sheltering rock, the vestige of a path tracing its way down towards the valley bottom.

Still pathless, I picked my way down to the lowest part of the depression and soon reached the faint path that I had half suspected would be there. The further I went, the more distinct the path became. I later found it described by Wainwright as a "drove road". The depression on the fellside, that isn't visible from the valley floor is, it seems, the area where wandering sheep were collected before being driven down to overwinter in the valley.

My descent by this path that reaches the road opposite the Borrowdale Gates hotel continued slowly, owing to the erratic buffeting of the wind, but I was delighted to have discovered what for me was an unexpected track, and I was back at my Borrowdale Hotel five hours after starting the walk. It had been a splendid day during which, not surprisingly, I saw nobody at all on the fell except the two young lads repairing the bridge over Tongue Gill.

Note: Having discovered the drove road track and finding myself in the area a year later, on a day of better weather, I used the track again and took the following photograph:

Grange in Borrowdale from the "drove road" on High Spy
March 28ᵗʰ 2019

DOVE'S NEST CRAG

I first came upon this crag while still a teenager in an anthology of short articles, the name of which I regret disappeared long ago into the dustbin of forgotten dreams. Nevertheless, I remembered a few details. The crag was apparently a useful place for rock climbers to visit when the weather wasn't fit for climbing owing to bad weather on the higher crags. It was formed when a massive rock face broke away from the mountainside to slide down and leave a pile of fragmented boulders leaning against the face behind. I supposed from this that it must be in a valley bottom somewhere. It was obvious to me that walkers, as well as climbers, might enjoy escaping from the rain inside its complicated interior.

The result of the landslide is a jumble of cavities waiting to be explored by any curious climber or walker. I also knew that it was located somewhere in Combe Gill, the valley that lies between the two great ridges that give Glaramara its imposing appearance when viewed from Borrowdale. The precise location, however, remained a mystery.

My first opportunity to locate it, admittedly at long range, was in June 1971, when I returned with Brenda to the Borrowdale Hotel for three nights and I led her up Glaramara from Seatoller. Both our girls were away on a school holiday. We followed the route described by Wainwright, so Combe Gill would be below us to our left, and although I scoured the flanks of Rosthwaite Fell on the far side using binoculars, I could see no trace of a substantial crag that might have been Dove's Nest. But it was a lovely day, so, nearing the summit, I led Brenda up what Wainwright refers to as a rock step that may be avoided. I was a little worried that she might have preferred the easier alternative, but she had no trouble and didn't even complain when, later, I decided to descend from Glaramara directly, and pathless, into Langstrath, at that time an unexplored valley for me.

On another occasion when I was climbing Glaramara alone (my second search), I encountered a timid lady at the foot of the rock step and had to persuade her that there would be no problem reaching the summit of Glaramara because the difficult step could be avoided. I was still looking for the crag and cast my search over a wider area but again failed to find it. Nearly fifty years passed before I tried again to locate the elusive cave, but I had chosen the worst possible day to climb Glaramara for a third time – it coincided with the arrival of Storm Ali in 2018 (described above). That day, I left Seatoller in good spirits well wrapped up in waterproofs to follow the familiar path, forgetting that I would be on the wrong side of Comb Gill. I should have paid more attention to the map before I turned off the Borrowdale road. I kept hoping for a bridge but there wasn't one. Furthermore, the stream was in full spate and any attempt to cross it would have been disastrous. Soon after I started, rain began to fall and an hour later was driving hard across the fell. I was drenched, cold and hungry, and with no chance of finding Dove's Nest on a distant fellside that was frequently obscured by sheets of rain, I abandoned the search in favour of a hot bath.

Less than a year later, in January 2019 I rented a cottage in Keswick to stay for a week with Rosalind and Adrian. Once more I planned to climb Glaramara should a day of suitable weather present itself and, if possible, get closer to Dove's Nest. Fortunately, one morning that week we woke to a cloudless sky above hard frozen ground and the weather forecast told us it would remain so all day. Adrian drove us to Seatoller where we parked the car as usual. Rosalind's golden retriever, Sophie, was with us. This time I intended to climb Glaramara by way of Rosthwaite Fell so we walked back along the road towards Rosthwaite further than usual and crossed the road bridge over Comb Gill before turning off the road.

For once we were on the same side of Comb Gill as the crag. We climbed steadily, trying to guess which of the crags above us would be the one. However, one by one they fell behind us and despite frequently referring to the map, we never found the crag. Basically, this was because the true reason for the walk was to climb Glaramara. Referring to the map at the end of the day, I realised that we had turned up towards the Rosthwaite Fell ridge about half a mile too soon and had climbed the true right bank of Rottenstone Gill as far as a body of water with the delightful name, Tarn at Leaves.

From the tarn, we headed south along a winding route amongst a confusion of rocky outcrops until we found an obvious sun trap and decided it was time for lunch. A solitary fell runner came racing past as we ate, and how I envied him his youth and fitness on a day that must surely have been stolen from heaven. Despite being a stranger to the area, Adrian led us unerringly across frozen bogs and hollows towards the foot of Wainwright's rock step. Rather than circumnavigate this I had a go at climbing it, but it was encased in so much ice that I was forced to follow in the footsteps of the others. All day long the sun had shone with a dazzling brilliance and never faltered as we turned north to descend, our shadows lengthening before us. Even bathed in the afternoon sun, I still failed to pick out the Crag on the far side of Comb Gill, but I vowed it would not be long before I returned.

Two months later, on March 26th 2019, I was back in Borrowdale with a single purpose in mind – to find and explore Dove's Nest Crag. I took the bus from the hotel to Seatoller and, having scoured the map, I knew the exact location and so for once, I had no worries about finding it. There is, however, one aspect of exploring new ground that is irritating but still provides a sense of achievement. Having almost reached the crag two months earlier, I naturally followed the same track and climbed to about 1,000 ft until, having crossed over Rottenstone Gill, the crag was clearly ahead of me. Unfortunately, the terrain on the steep fell side at that height holds a lot of loose scree and I could see that the base of the crag was much lower. It was hard work scrambling over the unstable rocks ensuring that I didn't have an accident. I had already experienced one broken femur and old age brings with it an army of complaints, one of which is an impaired sense of balance. I took a long time to descend to the level ground below the crag. But I had succeeded in reaching it at the fifth attempt.

With no one to guide me and with very little written information, the satisfaction that I felt was far greater than if I'd been led there by an experienced guide. Of course, I could have read more or asked more questions or, in this age of technology, used the internet. But as one of my favourite authors has said, and I paraphrase, 'It's the journey, not the arrival that matters.' Having arrived I made the most of being there alone, and wandered about the crag, inside and out, looking into various caverns and taking extra care not to have an accident while scrambling about. When I'd had enough, I descended to cross to the far side of Comb Gill and walked back on the far side of the valley to join the familiar Glaramara footpath. It had been a good day.

The entrance to North Cave, Dove's Nest Crag
March 29ᵗʰ 2019

The next day was even better. I was leaving for home, but the
Borrowdale Hotel has always allowed me to leave the car there. It
was a lovely Spring day, so I thought I might as well fit in a
morning climbing Catbells. When I reached the col between
Catbells and Maiden Moor, I was disappointed, though not really
surprised, to see that Catbells was too crowded for me, so I turned
south towards Maiden Moor. I soon came upon a couple having a
coffee break and stopped for a breather, having only a moment
earlier finished the climb to the col. I mentioned to them that the
day before I'd had a very good day on Dove's Nest Crag and asked
if they knew the crag.

'Yes, I know it,' replied John, for that was his name. 'I've
climbed there.'

'Well,' I told him, 'you're the first person I've met who's even
heard of it. I'm trying to get fit for a trip to Scotland in May.'

'There's a coincidence,' he said. 'We're going to Scotland in May. Where are you staying?'

'We've booked a cottage close to Lochinver,' I told him. 'I'm hoping to climb Suilven.'

'Not another coincidence!' he smiled. 'That's why we are going, but we'll be staying on the southern side.'

The coincidences went on and on as we discovered that our holidays would overlap and that he, like me, was aged 82.

I said I'd look out for them – John and Rosemary. When I left them, I continued my walk following the path that skirts the rim of the crags overlooking the Newlands Valley. I saw them briefly once more, some distance behind me before I descended from High Spy to use the drove road that I'd discovered the year before when I'd sought refuge from Storm Ali. Again, I'd enjoyed another great day on the fells.

Catbells and Skiddaw from Maiden Moor
March 29ᵗʰ 2019

SUILVEN – ONE LAST MOUNTAIN

In May 2019, I went to Scotland with Rosalind, Kathryn and Rosalind's partner, Adrian, to climb Suilven, an iconic mountain that stands alone, as do many of the mountains of Assynt in Scotland's far North-West. Unlike the Munros of Torridon or the Central Highlands, these mountains give the impression that they never speak to each other. There are no connecting ridges so, unless you are a superman, they must be climbed one at a time. Suilven for instance lies so far from a motor road that a five mile walk is needed before one reaches the foot of the mountain. And that's where the real climbing begins.

The cottage that I rented for a week was situated at Torbreck, two miles out of Lochinver, the nearest town to our mountain. It was a delight to sit there in the evenings and watch the deer that came down from the hills to graze on the lawns as the sun went down. Not wishing to miss out on the climb, Kathryn had come from New Zealand and, together with Rosalind and Adrian, not forgetting Sophie, Rosalind's golden retriever, we had a superb holiday. On the first day, we drove to Achmellvich Bay from where we walked by heather tracks amidst a waste of rocks and tumbling streams to Altnabradhan Mill and Cove. As if that wasn't enough, we went on that same day to the Stoer lighthouse to follow the cliff track for views of the Old Man of Stoer. We returned by way of Sidhean Mor, an elevated area of moorland that gave us a tremendous view of the Assynt giants standing out in glorious isolation; each one appearing to be defiant, proud and challenging. It was a long day for me, so I was glad for the easier day that followed when we spent a gentle half-day walking through Glen Canisp.

I knew that climbing Suilven would be a long day. Most writers seem to consider that eight hours is a reasonable time, so we were up early enough to have everything ready to leave our two cars at 8.45am at a small car park on the Canisp Lodge Road. This saved us some distance and height than if we'd had to start the walk from

Lochinver. The track beyond Canisp Lodge that could be used by a 4 x 4, seemed to go on forever, and I thought my progress might prove to be too slow when I was overtaken by a few other walkers. Mountain bikers I didn't mind, and I even wished I'd thought myself about hiring a bike for the day.

Suilven from a lochan beside the long walk in.
The ascent climbs to the saddle between the two peaks.
Caisteal Liath is on the right
May 14th 2019

Rosalind and Adrian would advance now and then and wait for me to catch up while Sophie investigated various smells or found a lochan from which to have a drink. For most of the time, Kathryn stayed chatting to me and the time passed easily enough as the track rose and fell and wound its way towards a footbridge that we reached in well under two hours. Soon after that, the serious climbing began at a point where an obvious footpath diverges from the main track. This rises gradually across the remaining moorland over a series of shallow layered escarpments as far as the foot of the mountain.

Looking east to Meall Meadhonach from Caisteal Liath

On the final steep ascent to the saddle, I had to rest many times, but the climb was well worth the effort as I breasted the ridge at its lowest point between Suilven's two summits. At that point there is a sudden view of Stac Polly to the south which I'd read about and was expecting. Nevertheless, it revived nostalgic memories of when I'd climbed it thirty years earlier with Brenda. We rested there for lunch before continuing to the summit of Caisteal Liath about 500 ft higher, needing to use our hands occasionally, and certainly to help Sophie.

Being such an isolated mountain, the view from the summit is extensive, giving a full 360° without interruption, although I had to walk to the west end to be able to look down towards Lochinver.

There is no safe way off the summit except back to the col from where a dedicated collector of summits would include Meall Meadhonach, the other peak seen in the photo. But I was content and offered to wait if the rest of the party wished to climb it, but they declined, and we followed the ascent route in reverse back to the car which we reached exactly eight hours after leaving it.

The next day I went out with Kathryn for a meal. I knew that John and Rosemary should have arrived, so I was looking out for them. Before we had finished our main course, a couple came in and sat behind Kathryn who was sitting facing me. I wondered – is it or is it not the friends I'd met on Maiden Moor in March. Then they had been well wrapped up in climbing/walking gear but here they were in everyday clothes. We had soon finished eating but I had to be sure, so I waited until the lady got up and went to pay, at which point I went across and said tentatively. 'Excuse me but I'm looking for a couple I met earlier this year – John and Rosemary.'

'Well,' he answered, I'm John, and that's Rosemary. She's just gone to pay the bill.'

When Rosemary joined us she asked me if I'd climbed Suilven, and of course I had to answer 'Yes,' whereupon she asked if it had been hard and did I think she would manage it. I gave her the only answer I could think of.

'Yes, it was very hard, but if you're determined, you'll manage it.' I do hope she did.

[Now I must apologise for referring to Suilven as my last mountain, because any perceptive reader may remember, that when I walked round North Wales in 1956 as described earlier, I referred to another ascent of Cnicht that I would make sixty-five years later. This I did in May 2021, following my frustration at being locked down for over a year by Covid-19. The cottage that I rented for a week at Nantmor, near Beddgelert was within walking distance of Cnicht – and also close to the one-time youth hostel at Cae Dafydd where, in 1956, I'd stayed with my cousin, John.]

BACK TO SCHOOL

Ever since I was privileged to attend the Outward Bound Mountain School at Ullswater, I've kept in touch with the Outward Bound movement, even to taking Brenda for a visit during our Borrowdale honeymoon! If we were ever on holiday in Eskdale and it coincided with the Eskdale Fête, we would both happily spend an afternoon at the Eskdale OBMS. On one occasion a ceilidh band was playing country dance music. Nobody seemed willing to get out of their chairs, so when the compere asked for volunteers to dance a Cumberland Square Eight, Brenda and I were up straight away. Nobody else joined in, so the compere asked us where we were from, and when we told him Wigan, he felt compelled to address the crowd and denigrate them for needing two "foreigners" to teach native Cumbrians their own dance.

Twice I've accepted invitations, as an elderly adult, to join a walk over Helvellyn led by members of the Ullswater school staff. At the first of these I was invited to sign the "Roll of Honour". Brenda and I decided to make a weekend of it and stayed in Keswick for three nights. On the Saturday Brenda dropped me off at the school and drove into Penrith to do some shopping. Once the introductions and signings were over, it was 10.00am before we set off, led by two girls who were young enough to have been my granddaughters. On that occasion, I came as near to witnessing a fatal accident as I have ever been. The school had provided transport for, I suppose, about ten alumni and their spouses or partners to be driven to Glenridding. From there, by way of Greenside Mines, we would be taken over Helvellyn by way of Red Tarn and Striding Edge, returning by Swirral Edge – a standard circuit for many walkers. It wasn't the best of days for weather with the higher fells in cloud and intermittent rain falling lower down, so we knew that Striding Edge would be treacherous. I was pleasantly surprised to find that I wasn't the slowest member of the party, which had been a worry to me before we set off. However, I found the (relatively) long halts quite relaxing and a reminder for me of the virtue of being patient, so for once I was careful not to rush off ahead of the "team".

If you've read the preceding chapters diligently, you may guess by now that once we reached Striding Edge, I chose to follow the top of the ridge rather than use the safer path just below it on the Red Tarn side. The whole length of the Edge was in cloud, and as we neared its junction with Helvellyn we heard a shout ahead of us. Everywhere was shrouded in mist, so we only learned, when we caught up with a party that had passed us a few minutes earlier, that one of them had fallen from the ridge crest to finish up close to Red Tarn about 500 ft below. There was a doctor at the scene, and they had reported the accident, so a helicopter was on its way. Within 10 or 15 minutes we heard the noise of the helicopter but had no idea where it was until a flashing light below us in the depths of Nethermost Cove gave its location away. It ascended towards us slowly, its light flashing through the mist until it hovered closely above us. The sound of its rotors was deafening and frightening as it swayed in the turbulence, and we all pointed frantically down to where the casualty and his support party were waiting. It seemed an age before the pilot deemed it safe to descend to Red Tarn, which had now become visible, probably due to the down draught of the rotors thinning the mist. Happy that the casualty would now be in safe hands we resumed our walk over Helvellyn with lunch taken at the summit shelter. When we reached Greenside on our return, we discovered from a chance contact who was known to the girls, that the casualty, although conscious by the side of Red Tarn, had sadly died on his way to Carlisle hospital.

That same weekend, knowing that Brenda would enjoy a gentle stroll, I took her through Brundholme Woods towards Blencathra and over Latrigg from the east. On the way home she was kind to me and dropped me off late in the day at Stonethwaite, having arranged to meet me at the New Dungeon Ghyll hotel in Langdale. I planned to go by way of Langstrath and the Stake Pass but couldn't resist including Pike o' Stickle, which I had all to myself. I had a quick look around the stone axe factory area, but found nothing of interest, and then descended by way of the great stone shoot which I soon realised was a mistake for it seemed to take forever, being far more broken up than I remembered.

A year later, in September 2005, the Ullswater OBMS celebrated its 50th anniversary with another guided walk to Helvellyn's summit, so once again we booked ourselves in to High Hill Farm in Keswick where we had stayed many times. On this occasion we left the school later than I supposed the leaders had intended, and we climbed Helvellyn from Patterdale by Red Tarn and Swirral Edge without incident. A celebration had been arranged at the school, but we were back too late to hear the speeches and witness the celebratory cake cutting. Brenda, on the other hand, having expected us all to be back from our walk earlier, had enjoyed the whole event.

In June 2019, any interested alumni were invited back to learn about the many improvements that have been made over the years and, if they desired, to participate in some of the well-remembered activities of their youth, such as canoeing or having an early morning dip in the lake. But more of that later.

This again was too good an invitation to miss, although it would be nothing like my two earlier visits, so I booked myself into the Borrowdale Hotel for two nights. I arrived at the hotel before mid-day and my room was ready, so that gave me an afternoon to go exploring. I made a quick change into shirt and shorts and walked the half mile or so into Troutdale to Black Crag. Having once climbed Troutdale Pinnacle many years before, I'd forgotten how much scrambling up moss covered boulders I had to do before I even reached the foot of the crag. Three ropes of climbers were already on the crag, so I didn't approach too closely to search for the start of the Pinnacle climb, though I did mention to them that I'd climbed it about fifty years earlier. I watched them for a while but saw little progress, although there was much shouting from someone out of sight above a bulge. I then climbed up alongside the crag on its right-hand side using a path by which climbers descend before they make another ascent of the crag by a different route. After a visit to the top of the Pinnacle to remind myself of its vertigo inducing verticality by peering over the edge of the crag,

I set off to explore the trackless hinterland, hoping to reach either the Watendlath road or the Ashness Woods path back to the hotel.

This was truly wild country – not even sheep bother to go there. Bracken was waist high and where it petered out, heather hid the ground below. Wherever a slope showed promise of descending to the Watendlath road, invariably I encountered an unseen (from above) impassable crag – or if passable, then not advisable for an elderly solitary explorer. There was much retracing of my route which involved more climbing than I'd expected. The distance as the crow flies is little more than a mile or so, but the diversions and back tracking that I had to do before I reached the familiar footpath down to High Lodore took me three hours. The views, however, were sublime, especially glimpses of Skiddaw and Derwentwater that would appear when least expected from behind a rocky outcrop or half hidden through a grove of ash trees.

The next day after breakfast I had a late start and took the Borrowdale bus to the Stonethwaite junction to climb Eagle Crag, using Wainwright to guide me across the face of the crag. I had first seen Eagle Crag during my youth hostelling circuit of the Lakes in 1955 with my cousin John and had, on many occasions since, thought what a good climb it would be for a short day. But every time there had been far more desirable climbs to tempt me. Seen from Stonethwaite Beck, Eagle Crag presents a seemingly impregnable wall of vertical rock, but behind that impressive façade lies an easy grassy ridge descending from the Lake District's central plateau of High Raise by way of Sergeant's Crag. Such a broad ridge has never had much attraction for me, but I'd been re-reading Wainwright's account of Eagle Crag and found that he describes an ascending route through those forbidding rocks. Probably I may have read it once and then laid it aside for so long that I'd forgotten all about it. Anyway, this was the day to visit another place where I'd never been.

I'd chosen the Stonethwaite bus stop because I was tired of using the path from Rosthwaite on the other side of the river; I'd normally used that as a starting point to walk or run from Borrowdale to meet Brenda in Grasmere or Langdale. This time I'd use it for the return journey. As I passed the church, I recalled the last time I'd attended worship there with Brenda. After the service, having an interest in pipe organs, I'd stayed behind to chat with the organist. Meanwhile, as she waited for me, Brenda was engaged in conversation with the vicar, Gay Pye, the result being that Gay invited us to the vicarage for tea and biscuits (sadly not the fatted calf that she had referred to in her sermon).

Beyond the bridge at Stonethwaite where the road ends, the track shares the route of the Borrowdale fell race for a couple of hundred yards before the latter breaks off to the right to climb through the steep wooded slopes of Bessyboot. It was a good warm day again, so I'd set off in T-shirt and shorts without taking any wet weather gear. But as I approached the first bridge in Langstrath, the sky darkened and was threatening rain, so I had to make a decision. I'd taken the Langstrath route because I wanted to walk round the base of Eagle Crag on a path I'd never used before. Also, I reasoned it would give me more time to decide what to do if the weather were to break. By the time I'd reached the footbridge and gate that allowed me to back track to the Greenup Edge path on the far side of Langstrath Beck, the skies had brightened and the rest of the day was fine and dry.

Wainwright shows paths on both sides of Greenup Gill, but he doesn't mention that there is a fence on the true left side. Because I didn't want to ascend too far without having an opportunity to cross over, I used the path on the same side of the Gill as the crag and above the fence. I found it much more difficult than the Greenup Edge path on the far bank that I knew well. I supposed that hardly anyone goes that way, but by using it I could begin the serious part of the climb whenever I thought it would be appropriate. Eventually, after crossing a wall separating the pathless hillside from the crag, a steady climb up steep grassy slopes brought me to the semblance of a path. This soon turned into one that was easy to follow as it contoured below the crags using a series of terraces to gain height. I had no trouble with stopping many times to admire the tremendous views down the valley, although at one point I followed a false trail to my right that led me to the top of a vertical precipice. That short path was distinct enough to suggest that others before me had made the same mistake. I was soon on the summit however, which, as I hoped and expected, I had to myself.

Reunion by Eagle Crag

Across the deep ravine of Greenup Ghyll,
fingers of mist were fondling ferns
while water spilled from hollow caves
amongst a waste of broken rock.
Somewhere the bleating of a lamb was painting
fear on the canvas of the mountainside,
the only sound that rode the wind.
Concerned, I stopped my climb, but
searched in vain until a rattle of stones
disturbed the peace. A black lamb,
lost below the shadow of a crag,
moved stiff-legged, lost and jerkily searching.
Across the valley depth I heard
far off a deeper foreign voice, distressed.
Each spoke to each as over rocks and tumbling
streams, love's magnet drew them in.
Then silence, and I knew, though never saw
why nuzzling lamb and worried Herdwick
suddenly were dumb.

I descended by what you might call Eagle Crag's "back door", heading south-east towards Greenup Gill where I met the first people I'd seen all day. I'd watched them in the distance as I descended, and guessed that they were coming over from Grasmere. They stopped occasionally, I supposed, to check their whereabouts on the map. I was enjoying my solitary walk so I also stopped, but at a point where I could refresh myself with a drink from Greenup Gill well below the path. I waited until they'd passed above me but they stopped again lower down at a gate, where I caught up with them to find that they had the map out. When I asked what they were doing, they told me they were on the last leg of their Duke of Edinburgh's gold award and were heading for the camp site at Stonethwaite. I congratulated them and they asked what I'd been doing and where I'd been. When I said, 'I've just been over that fell there,' pointing to Eagle Crag, they were suitably impressed.

The tidy crest of Eagle Crag
overlooking the Stonethwaite valley
June 19th 2019

That moment took me back to a day almost seventy years earlier when, as a teenager, I'd encountered an elderly gentleman who'd impressed me in a similar manner, and I couldn't help but envy those young lads the years ahead of them and all the hills that one day they'll discover and climb themselves.

The next day I left Borrowdale for The Inn on The Lake on Ullswater to spend one night there with other OBMS alumni. There were fifteen of us, together with three wives. After a brief lunch we were all taken across the lake by Zodiak to the Outward Bound development at Howtown that began in 2008. There we learned that the OBMS arrangements for introducing young people to the adventure of the "Great Outdoors" are today vastly different from those that I experienced over sixty years ago.

We returned to the main centre for a debriefing of our time there and also to talk and share nostalgically about what we had learned while there. We were each given our teenage "end of term report" which some of us saw in its entirety for the first time. Rain set in as we returned to the hotel for our evening meal, and there was much more chatting before we all retired to bed, well satisfied with a stimulating day.

The next morning, we were collected again by minibus to return to the school where those who wished went canoeing, while the others who had volunteered for the "jog and dip" had the procedure explained to them. This bore little relationship with that of my experience years ago when ninety-six young lads assembled on the school yard at 6.00am every morning and ran down to the lake to strip off naked for a full immersion before running back for a hot shower.

We were now "participants" rather than guests, and so were required to obey the school rules, meaning that we had to wear shorts (on top of the "speedos" which I normally use and was already wearing for modesty), a top body cover and also a buoyancy aid tightly strapped on. Furthermore, although it was by now after 10.00am, to avoid thermal shock, we had to immerse ourselves gradually before we jumped into the lake from the jetty. Nor was diving permitted despite the depth being, in my opinion, adequately safe. Perhaps it was as well, although I hadn't really looked forward to having a naked dip. I also understood the need to avoid vagal inhibition that might induce a tragic and unnecessary death amongst we aged pensioners. In any case there were several young girls nearby testing their abilities on a climbing frame. The dip was followed by a run (or in my case a swift walk) back to the school for the usual hot shower. There was still time left for questions and discussion before we enjoyed a light lunch and a walk down to the old boathouse. I left again that day with more happy memories of the Ullswater school to add to my already bulging pack.

REFLECTIONS

Today, when I go for a walk, either close to home, or among mountains or by the sea, I invariably come across litter that reminds me of those words by the hymn writer Reginald Heber that '*every prospect pleases and only man is vile.*' It saddens me that as more and more people discover the pleasures of climbing hills and mountains or exploring any wilderness in search of adventure, the more those hills, mountains and wildernesses become less desirable. All walkers and climbers are exhorted to "take only photographs, leave only footprints" and I'm sure that the vast majority do, yet litter may be found on any path you take on any hill, by any lake, or on any shore.

After seventy years of exploration amongst the hills and mountains of Britain, I now find myself in two minds. While I recognise that wild country induces a calmness of spirit to troubled minds and can be a route for many people to escape from the stresses of everyday life, I'm seldom pleased when I meet a laughing band of happy wanderers nowadays because I can remember a time when it seemed I had the fells almost to myself.

I know that sounds as if I would like it to be so forever, and much as I admire the blessed Alfred Wainwright (A.W) for his magnificent hand-drawn guides to the Lakeland Fells – I've used them myself and I even own two of his original drawings, I can't help but worry about the thousands of people who now crowd the summits of the central fells, because he's been their guide and mentor. For my first walk with my cousin, John, round the Lake District in 1955, I used no more than a Ward Lock Lake District guidebook and knowledge amassed from my own reading, in much the same way that A.W. himself would have done, perhaps influenced by reading *Walking In The Lake District* by the Revd Herbert Henry Symonds, one of my favourite books during my teenage years.

We all know that the hills are eternal, yet their face has changed since 1955 when, like A.W himself before me, I first stood on Orrest Head to marvel at the saw-toothed ridges of the hills that defined the Western skyline. Those were places waiting for me to explore and there were tracks to follow then. Mostly they were narrow and many, but not all of them, in my ignorance would lead me to where I wished to go. I had much to learn. Since then, over the years I have seen many paths becoming wider, especially those that lead to popular summits or include stretches of boggy ground where walkers have strayed to the side in search of drier ground. Because of this, "Fix The Fells" was born in 2021 with funding from the Heritage Lottery Fund to repair and maintain paths that were perceived to have become a scar on the landscape. Much research and skill has gone into creating rocky staircases and to improving paths to allow disabled access, all of which is both admirable and commendable, but I can't help thinking that in so doing, we are in danger of destroying the very reason why we visit such places.

But then, I have to admit that we have exploited the Lake District for centuries. We have mined for copper at Coniston and for lead at Glenridding. Slate from the Honister quarries is renowned the world over. Carrock Fell is still invaded by seekers after minerals and I have myself found traces of malachite, an ore of copper, below the north face of Dalehead. Even the relative remoteness of the Newlands valley was exploited by German miners, imported during the C16th on behalf of Queen Elizabeth. Today, Tilberthwaite would be at best a wasteland, and at worst an eyesore, were it not for the woodlands that now disguise the ravaged landscape left by extensive quarrying. Many years ago, I came across a rusting knapping machine (used for breaking rocks into smaller ones), standing forlornly and deserted a little way off the footpath from High Tilberthwaite to Little Langdale. The last time I went that way it had disappeared, (or maybe I had forgotten the path). I hope it has found its way to a suitable museum of industry.

All over the region, you will find evidence of human activity; fell walking is but one more. In a different context, Oscar Wilde wrote that "Each man kills the thing he loves." The Lake District is without doubt one of the most beautiful places on earth and is loved by so many people that it is in danger of being killed, or at least mutilated, by the millions of feet of those who love it. The very essence of a wilderness is lost when it is invaded by so many people that it becomes no longer a wilderness. Almost two hundred years ago, Wordsworth fumed against the railway that was planned to bring hordes of tourists to his beloved Vale of Grasmere. Even then, I think he could see what the future held for that blessed plot. But today, we have the National Trust, The Friends of the Lake District, The Campaign to Protect Rural England and Fix The Fells, not to mention scores of local authorities, each in its own way doing its best to care for and protect the natural environment and Britain's wild places.

But consider for a moment the buildings and other remaining evidence of the industry that once disfigured the landscape of Coppermines Valley at Coniston and can still be traced there. If the valley were today in the pristine state that nature intended before it was destroyed by human activity, do you think that planning permission for such activity would be allowed? Yet we allow the tourist industry to flourish and even encourage it by constructing staircases to mountain tops. Maybe I'm going over the top there (sorry about the pun) but I trust you get my drift.

During my lifetime, the world population has more than tripled. More and more people are seeking not only food to survive, but also space in which to live and eat. The pressures on the wilderness and on wild places in which to accommodate them continues to grow without any sign of diminishing. The honeypots of the Lake District, North Wales and Scotland today draw hordes of tourists, or should I say visitors, many of them day trippers. In summer, the streets of Bowness, Ambleside and Keswick resemble Blackpool's Golden Mile on a Bank Holiday, and cars heading for such places queue nose to tail for miles. Then, when they arrive, they find nowhere to park. On the other hand, residents need these visitors, for there is little other work to be had.

I do not envy the policy makers who must decide the best way forward for these beautiful areas. There are hard choices to be made and not everyone will agree what is best. I only know that I seldom go now to the central fells of the Lake District, especially in summer, because there are other places that I know where I can find peace and be alone if I wish.

So, what will the future hold for those who come after us, seeking to find for themselves the joys we knew? If I extrapolate the changes that I have witnessed in my lifetime, (and I write here only of the Lake District because that's the area I know best), I can foresee a time when access to the fells, in particular the central fells, will of necessity need to be limited. If it's true that 200,000 pairs of feet climb Scafell Pike annually, it's no wonder that paths become eroded and accidents happen more frequently, and in doing so place an ever-increasing demand on the mountain rescue services.

A climb to the top of a 3,000 ft mountain is not a stroll in the park. The free access that has for so long been admired and regarded as a personal right is under threat and, projecting my own observations into the future, there may come a day when tolls are placed on the major roads into the area and ticket booths erected at the start of popular ascents to the major summits. In recent years, some fell races have become so popular that the numbers permitted to enter are now limited, so it's no good turning up at the start without booking your place in advance. God forbid that this ever happens to our freedom to roam, but it may happen one day. How long will it be before you go for a walk with a damnation of drones buzzing about your head, keeping their private eyes locked on you? Equipment will be checked and anyone without a map, compass, whistle or spare food and clothing etc. will be barred from continuing.

That may be a nightmare scenario, but mountain country, either here or abroad has attracted tourists ever since the first inquisitive travellers such as Celia Fiennes and Daniel Defoe wrote their accounts of these magical areas. Recently, nothing has distressed me more than a photograph of climbers, queueing to reach the summit of Everest having to step over the bodies of those who had died because their oxygen had run out through waiting too long for their turn to take another step. This, even though access to the mountain must be booked in advance and permission given by the Nepalese government. I see nothing ahead to convince me that tourism will not continue to increase, probably at an ever-increasing rate. But there are many places in these delectable islands of ours, other than the Lake District and the other National Parks, that are equally worthy of exploration. In fact, I know places within the Lake District boundaries where one may find solitude, but I'm not going to name them – I've already said enough. It's up to you, the individual, to seek them out and find them for yourself, much as I did seventy years ago in those blessed years when I was young and green.

Finally, I wish those readers who've read this far a long, happy and safe life of walking, climbing, exploring or doing whatever turns them on amongst the wild and beautiful places that enrich these crowded islands of ours. And I promise, that if I should, by chance, come across you on a quiet, secluded path, I'll greet you with a smile and wish you well.

Climbing the Graph

Why is the gift-wrapped hope
of age so prized amongst
the very young? Can they not wait?
They count their Christmases
impatiently until one day they find
they'd like to have them back.

We elderly who slalom
down the right side of the
Gaussian skewed graph
of life have not grown old. We know
our journey hasn't flat lined yet

although,
like all the young, we climbed in haste
the statistician's ogive
steepness to its peak, and there
contentedly relaxed.

But there's no getting off
the curve, and so we live in hope
we'll find more hills to climb
before we settle down upon
the endless waiting plain.

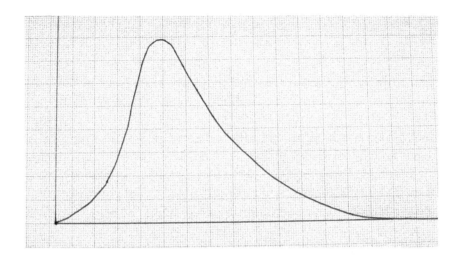

POSTSCRIPT

The outbreak of the coronavirus pandemic at the start of 2020 put an end to many people's holiday plans, including mine. My planned week in a cottage near Beddgelert in May with Rosalind and Adrian would have to be postponed for an indefinite period. At that stage I had decided that Suilven would have been my last mountain, so I was resigned to the fact that my climbing days were at an end. But fate moves in mysterious ways, and we were able to have our holiday a year later in 2021, again in May when the lockdown regulations were to some extent more relaxed. The fact that the cottage was within walking distance of the beautiful little peak of Cnicht was too tempting for me to miss. Known as the "Welsh Matterhorn" on account of its triangular appearance when seen from the area around Porthmadog, Cnicht is really no more than the end of a roughly horizontal ridge.

I chose to climb it with Rosalind on a fine day when a light wind was blowing. Adrian drove us to our starting point from the village car park in Croesor and then took Sophie, the dog, for a gentler walk, even though she had accompanied us to the summit of Suilven two years earlier. Cnicht is not a great mountain but there is more to a good walk than merely ascending the highest peak around. I guessed that Snowdon summit would have been crowded on such a glorious day, so I was delighted that we encountered few other walkers all day.

Leaving Croesor, the approach to the end of the Cnicht ridge begins with a steep but short stretch of road at the end of which a right turn brings the walker on to the mountain itself. The rising path continues across varied terrain involving stretches of scree and rough pasture. Eventually, nearing the summit there is enough scrambling to excite the spirit of any aging adventurer, not to mention the superb views of Tremadog Bay beyond Porthmadog, the Lleyn peninsula and the rugged texture of the closer broken ground stretching away towards Snowdon. The wind was light but strong enough to dapple the hillsides with a delightful and ever changing tapestry of light and shade from the several broken clouds floating above.

Thus it was that Cnicht replaced Suilven as my last mountain. It will undoubtedly remain so because on December 7th 2021, I tripped in my garage and sustained a second, and more serious, fracture to my left femur – the same one that had been repaired twelve years earlier with a titanium prosthesis. Following that first fracture, being aware of the enhanced fragility of my left leg, I had always been careful to ensure that when climbing on potentially dangerous ground, I took no unnecessary risks. I even condescended to accept that I needed to use a walking stick because I knew that my balance was impaired. When I fell in the garage, I had effectively completed this book, prior to publication. To sustain another such life-changing injury in a domestic situation, I thought, was the ultimate irony and must surely be the end of all my aspirations for future walks, however modest they might be. I spent eighteen days in hospital on my back as my muscles and strength wasted away and I returned home on Christmas Eve, five days after undergoing major surgery to repair damage that was complicated by the earlier repair. As I write, I know that recovery is progressing well, although more slowly than I could wish. However, there is nothing to be gained by thinking, 'If only…' so I meet every day with hope and patience, resigned to knowing that I can no longer climb the high hills, although some of Wainwright's "Outlying Fells" may be within my reach. How much remains for me in the future I don't know, but I have a lifetime of memories to sustain me, and I return, as I often do, to the closing lines of Tennyson's *Ulysses* from which the final line has been adopted (with a minor change) by the Outward Bound Trust to which I dedicate this book, together with whatever finances accrue from its sales.

"…and tho'
We are not now that strength which in old days
Moved earth and heaven; that which we are; we are;
One equal temper of heroic hearts,
Made weak by time and fate, but strong in will
To strive, to seek, to find. And not to yield."

ABOUT THE AUTHOR

David Lythgoe was born in Wigan in 1937. He left Wigan Grammar School in 1954 after taking "A" level GCE to begin work as a student chemist with the (then) British Electricity Authority. He continued his education on a part-time basis, eventually acquiring a PhD in chemistry.

In 1987, he accepted a twelve-month appointment to work in India as a consultant on power station chemistry. While there, he began writing poems, some of which have appeared in the *Daily Telegraph* (one was commended by Andrew Motion, then poet laureate) and the *Methodist Recorder*. Since retiring in 1990, he has published three collections of poetry, some of which are included in the present work, and a comprehensive history of his local Methodist Church.

He was widowed in 2014 and is proud to have two happily married daughters.

ACKNOWLEDGEMENTS

I wish to thank the following for their assistance:

Dorothy Nelson for proof reading.

Gill and Martin James for advice and working with the photographs, some of which I took with a Kodak Brownie camera that dated back to the 1930s.

Michael Hunt for his appreciation of the contents.

Nick Barrett, Outward Bound CEO for writing the Foreword.

Rosalind and Adrian Smith for technical advice.

Alan Prosser for the cover design.

ALSO BY DAVID LYTHGOE

A House Nigh Unto Heaven
Travelling Light
Wigan Bred
Myrrh From The Forest